"*The Gathering Table* feels like a heart-to-heart visit with new friends. These women treasure community. As you try their recipes and read their insights, you'll be encouraged to connect in whatever way you can with the women in your life and find ways for your friendships to grow."

Robin Jones Gunn, bestselling author of *Becoming Us* in the Haven Makers series and the Father Christmas novels that inspired three Hallmark movies

"A hospitality handbook encouraging you to wholeheartedly welcome others to join you at your table. The Gingham Apron ladies demonstrate how to share the depth of our lives through gathering together. Their seasonal themed recipes, intentional applications, and meaningful traditions will inspire you to spend more time connecting and celebrating!"

Morgan Tyree, organizing expert, author of *Take Back Your Time* and *Your Hospitality Personality*, and founder of www.morganizewithme.com

"I have long followed and loved the work and hearts of the Gingham Apron girls, and I am thrilled they have captured the unfettered joy of their lives in this book. The recipes are vibrant and delicious, simple enough to tackle for dinner at home but equally perfect when we open our doors and set the table for a crowd. The accompanying stories and stunning photography make this the perfect addition to every cookbook shelf. *The Gathering Table* will be a beloved, dog-eared treasure for families looking to make their homes places where dear ones feel welcomed, seen, and deeply loved."

Kimberly Stuart, author of eight novels, including the Heidi Elliot series and *Heart Land*

"It's so easy to zip through life and forget to be intentional about quality family time. *The Gathering Table* is a beautiful collection of inspiring stories, lovely photographs, Bible truths, and recipes that help me remember why I want to gather my people around the table. This book is the reminder we all need in this fast-paced, busy world. It's a breath of fresh air for the soul."

Micah Maddox, women's event speaker and author of *Anchored In: Experience a Power-Full Life in a Problem-Filled World*

"Love should be the heartbeat of any get-together. *The Gathering Table* guides us by using remarkable stories, exquisite photos, and superb recipes that help us share the love of Christ with others. Hospitality is a powerful tool to further the gospel, and you will be inspired with each turn of the page."

Brenda Leavenworth, author of *Far Above Rubies*

"In *The Gathering Table*, the ladies of the Gingham Apron make readers feel they have taken a quick trip to Iowa and spent time on the farm talking about Jesus, the importance of relationships, and Grandma Betty's Key Lime Pie. This book calls us to linger together with good food and a great God."

Amy L. Sullivan, author of the picture book series Gutsy Girls: Strong Christian Women Who Impacted the World

The Gathering Table

GROWING STRONG RELATIONSHIPS
through FOOD, FAITH, and HOSPITALITY

THE GINGHAM APRON

Revell

a division of Baker Publishing Group
Grand Rapids, Michigan

© 2020 by The Gingham Apron, LLC

Published by Revell
a division of Baker Publishing Group
PO Box 6287, Grand Rapids, MI 49516-6287
www.revellbooks.com

Printed in the United States of America

Library of Congress Cataloging-in-Publication Data
Names: The Gingham Apron, LLC, author.
Title: The gathering table : growing strong relationships through food, faith, and hospitality / The Gingham Apron, LLC.
Description: Grand Rapids, Michigan : Revell, a division of Baker Publishing Group, 2020. | Includes index.
Identifiers: LCCN 2020006367 | ISBN 9780800737917 (cloth)
Subjects: LCSH: Hospitality—Religious aspects—Christianity. | Interpersonal relations—Religious aspects—Christianity. | Dinners and dining—Religious aspects—Christianity.
Classification: LCC BV4647.H67 G56 2020 | DDC 241/.671—dc23
LC record available at https://lccn.loc.gov/2020006367

The proprietor is represented by the literary agency of The Blythe Daniel Agency, Inc.

Principle photography by Katie Swanson Photography. Used by permission.

Photo on p. 8 by Two Sisters Photography. Used by permission.

All other photography by Annie Boyd, Shelby Herrick, Molly Herrick, and Denise Herrick.

Note: all temperatures are given in degrees Fahrenheit.

Interior design and typesetting by Brian Brunsting

20 21 22 23 24 25 26   7 6 5 4 3 2 1

We dedicate this book to

our family,

who has wholeheartedly
supported our endeavor
of gathering together.

Contents

Spring

Summer

Fall

Winter

Introduction

Oh, taste and see that the Lord is good!
Blessed is the man who takes refuge in him!

Ps. 34:8 ESV

One Sunday afternoon in late spring, as the bright green grass returned, the five of us gathered together on the farm with our families. The smell of lilacs greeted us, and beautiful bursts of pink peonies and roses welcomed us at the door. Farm life had awakened in full swing. Planting was finished, and the first cutting of hay was about to commence. We greeted each other with warm hugs and smiles. Cousins were ready to meet the new baby-bottle calves Grandpa kept in the barn. Once the welcomes and excitement quieted a bit, we gathered for another family meal, something we have done for years that naturally follows alongside our family business and farming lifestyle. Each of us generally contributes a favorite family recipe. The kids usually come away with a new song, craft, or game they've learned. We embrace the scenery and landscape of the current season of life.

After we finished our meal, we gals filled our coffee cups and headed into the living room. While sitting on the soft, pale yellow chairs, we leisurely discussed what seemed like an endless list of all of our favorite foods, and we realized just how many treasured family recipes we each brought to the table: Grandma Betty's Potato Salad and Key Lime Pie, and Grandma Maxine's Soft Ginger

Cookies and Peach Cobbler, just to name a few. We are a modern-day close-knit farm family, and each of these recipes comes with a special memory—and often a handwritten copy passed down through the generations.

As our conversation continued, we dreamed of making a cookbook to record our heritage as it is expressed through food. Because of our farming lifestyle and the Iowa climate, the four seasons are prominent in our lives; they envelop us and affect what we eat in each season. Also, the memories these foods carry can bring us back to a specific occasion, so we knew that our cookbook would also have to be reflective of the changing seasons—just like our lives.

Equally as prominent in our lifestyle are our family's strong ties to our faith—the foundation of our existence. God's plan of salvation through his Son, Jesus, is the imperative message not only for our family's future generations but also for our readers. We desire to cling to God's ways in our lifestyles and values, and we want to impress them upon our children throughout each day (Deut. 6:7). We could not write a book of family gatherings and recipes without also including our faith heritage.

What began as a simple conversation on that sunny Sunday afternoon soon became an intentional project. With faith, family, and seasons of life on our minds, we committed to plan, prepare, and collect writings from monthly gatherings throughout the course of an entire year. And so the year of gatherings began. The months came and went, and everyone in our family anticipated and started to love "the gatherings." The kids began asking, "What are we going to do next month?" The cousins started to get to know each other better, the communication among us five girls became more frequent, and we were becoming better friends, not just family. The men in our family also found themselves especially enjoying some wonderful food and fun locations too.

After turning this whimsical plan into reality, we were truly astonished by the many blessings that came from our "little cookbook project." It turned into rediscovering joy and fulfillment with God's vision for our relationships. Food and refreshment are just threads for connecting us; the gatherings are simply catalysts for cultivating strong families and relationships. God's design of hospitality, our acts of service, the love we show one another, and the pauses we take to make memories can have a profound impact on each one of us.

You, too, can bring your family, your church group, or your neighborhood closer together through meaningful yet simple meals and gatherings. Jesus often taught his twelve disciples around the table or around a fresh-caught meal on the beach. We have even been called to remember his perfect life and sacrifice for our sins through food elements—the bread and cup of communion. Something special happens when we gather, pause, and are refreshed by good food and conversation.

We Gingham Apron ladies hope to inspire you to gather around your tables— to slow down and embrace the richness of your relationships. We urge you to let go of the Pinterest-perfect ideas and instead honor God by seeking and initiating time with others to create meaningful moments and deepened relationships.

The Gingham Apron Ladies

Denise   Jenny   Shelby

Annie   Molly

What Gathering Means to Us

Meet the Authors

Annie

The kingdom of God is an upside-down sort of place where the smallest and simplest efforts can make the biggest impact. And that's the principle I've seen affirmed as our family has simply gathered together—our relationships and memories have been greatly increased and enriched. For this reason, gathering has come to mean working together to include the rich ways of God in our daily lives.

Shelby

Getting together with family and friends around my parents' table was a frequent theme of my childhood. As the world continues to change, I feel an even stronger pull to gather together with others. Throughout the years and with the shift of my role into that of wife and mother, the meaning of gathering has evolved. To me, it's less about the agenda or food and more about those simple yet significant moments that weave us together. Gathering around the table is one way I can answer God's call for us to grow our relationships with one another.

Molly

Gathering means intentionally connecting through our relationships by means of refreshment—this can be as modest as sipping coffee with a friend or as lavish as a full-spread dinner party. When we do this, we are showing those we love that we desire to be together, and we have set aside this moment just for them—because they are *worth* it! God loves each of us and calls us to share his love. Through this practice, we express our honor and devotion to him and one another, which fulfills and strengthens our relationships.

Denise

The tools in our toolboxes of food, drink, a lighted candle, perhaps a vase of flowers, and good conversation set the stage for our family gatherings, even after our one-year experiment. That invitation to come gather and the feeling of belonging it offers are *priceless*. Through this practice of hospitality, we exhibit our love for each other and show we are available, we listen, and we care. Relishing time spent with others, I am drawn in to listen and to share as a piece of life unfolds. In gathering, I desire to simply reflect Christ's love for us all.

Jenny

Gathering, to me, means getting together as a family, whether for fun or for something more serious. Gathering means important things are about to happen within our relationship building. We have the opportunity to build each other up in creative ways, to have real conversations and take time out to really get to know one another, and to help our family stay closely knit together. Encouragement is so helpful in our lives. More than anything, when our family gathers in one large group, it makes me think about how God loves us so much and how we show his love to each other. That's precious to me.

Spring

Family Picnic at the Park

Intentionally Unplugging

Strawberry Lemonade

Cucumber Dip

Tortellini Pasta Salad

Roast Beef Spread

Fresh Fruit with Almond Sugar in a Waffle Bowl

Strawberry Shortcake

It was a beautiful spring day when we gathered together for our family picnic at a local lake. This community lake is a perfect location for our family—with large grassy patches and mature shade trees lining the rock shore, we can easily throw some blankets on the ground and come together for our meal. A small playground with a big metal slide sits just steps away for the children to play, climb, and gain a bird's-eye glimpse of all the landscape just beginning to sprout its annual regrowth.

Spring in Iowa is when the weather begins to warm up and new life returns. The men in our family undertake their annual sprint to plant this year's crop in our fields. On this particular day, the sun was bright as it warmed our cheeks and the cool, gentle breeze reminded us of all the promises of spring. The kids played joyfully nearby; the girls went swinging on the playground and picked dandelions while the boys hatched a new plan to capture the geese lingering near the shoreline.

The day began to heat up as we managed to convince the kids to come to the blankets under the big shade trees for some lunch. We all sat together and enjoyed simple sandwiches and a few sides. The strawberry lemonade was extra popular and refreshing for the tiring kiddos. They soon caught a second wind and headed back out to explore the terrain while we cleaned up and moved out into the sun to enjoy its warmth and gain a better view of the activities and the scenery.

While we Gingham Apron ladies were planning our year of gatherings, we knew that with the arrival of spring we would want to plan something outdoors. We looked forward to the opportunity to enjoy the warmer days ahead and appreciate the beauty of the season. We also knew the urges to be on technology and the example we wanted to set for our children. We decided ahead of time to disconnect from our devices for the gathering that afternoon and deliberately engage with the people we were with and our natural surroundings.

As Christians, we try to be intentional in our walk with the Lord; we desire a close relationship with him. Just as we seek intentionality in our walk with the Lord—by reading our Bibles, attending church, and so forth—we also need to be intentional in our relationships with others.

In our ever-changing world of technology, we have this amazing ability right at our fingertips to be globally connected. But being plugged in with so little effort makes it easy to stop being present with the people around us. As much as technology connects us, it also can isolate and *disconnect* us. Technology and social media can actually leave us feeling inadequate or unworthy and longing for a true connection—human connection to real and authentic people.

What would it look like if we were to answer the command of loving our neighbor as ourselves (Luke 10:27) and try to be just as intentional in our relationships with others as we are with the Lord? To me that would mean letting go of the distractions and fully embracing the people I am with, in part by putting my phone away while at dinner, remaining focused on our conversation, and inquiring about what is going on in others' lives. I would make them a priority, and once plans were set, I would stick to them. I would be sure to listen closely before speaking and show them respect.

Our relationships with each other are a backbone of what we were made for. God gave us relationships to teach us how to mirror the kind of connection he wants with us. Our earthly relationships teach us. We grow from them, and we gain experiences that can strengthen our relationship with God and also encourage those around us to grow in their own walks with him.

Gathering outside together for a picnic without modern technology was a great reminder to take a deep breath and just slow down. We enjoyed the small moments, connected with each other, and soaked in the beauty of our surroundings. The day was a wonderful opportunity to be intentional and fulfill our mission of building relationships out among God's beautiful creation.

A Place at His Table

Annie

Did you know that David wrote down Psalm 23, reflecting on nature and on being a shepherd, when he was already the king of Israel? Charles Spurgeon wrote, "I like to recall the fact that this Psalm was probably written by David when he was a king. He had been a shepherd, and he was not ashamed of his former occupation."[1]

This was so impactful for me. Just think about it: as king, David was now rich, he lived in a palace, he had servants and treasures, and he was famous throughout his nation. Gone were his lowly days of sleeping with stinky sheep on chilly, dark, dangerous hillsides. But when he wanted to convey the messages of rest and restoration, peace and guidance, he wrote about *green pastures* and *still waters*.

I've always loved Psalm 23. As a farm girl, when I picture a green pasture, I remember walks to our pond, riding horses and four-wheelers, and even checking on calves with my dad in the pastures of our farm. I know firsthand that pastures are places of beauty and quiet peace. And I know that one of the reasons I loved our picnic at the park so much was that we were able to gather outside on a lovely, calm, green, grassy knoll.

I also treasure the image of still waters. I remember playing with my brothers in the creek behind our house, fishing, and floating on innertubes on our pond. And now, I think about going with my kids to visit the serene lake that borders my parents' farm. Still waters are refreshing and restorative to my mind and well-being. During our picnic afternoon, the sunlight sparkled on and birds flew over the quiet lake nearby.

David's metaphors of green pastures and still waters powerfully direct us to the impact of nature on our lives. Think about this: How does spending time in nature truly affect us? How does it help us to know God better and have more of him in our lives?

God's Creativity

> *The heavens declare the glory of God;*
> *the skies proclaim the work of his hands. (Ps. 19:1)*

Just think about God's handiwork, his craftsmanship—the minute details he put into every living tree, delicate flower, and variegated blade of grass. I once read a science book to my kids that taught us how there are over ten thousand species of fish in the sea. Just fish! God's creativity is infinite, and when I spend time outside, I feel compelled to praise him.

God's Power

Listen to this, Job;
    stop and consider God's wonders.
Do you know how God controls the clouds
    and makes his lightning flash?
Do you know how the clouds hang poised,
    those wonders of him who has perfect knowledge? (Job 37:14–16)

When I go outside, when I am still and stop to consider the wonders around me, I am reminded that God is infinitely wise. He has made all things; he is holding all things together (Col. 1:17). When I ponder the systems and seasons and remember that he is at work in it all, I am reminded that he can hold everything together in my life too. He knows what's best. His ways are perfect. This comforts me and gives me hope.

God's Sovereignty

But ask the animals, and they will teach you,
    or the birds in the sky, and they will tell you;
or speak to the earth, and it will teach you,
    or let the fish in the sea inform you.
Which of all these does not know
    that the hand of the LORD has done this?
In his hand is the life of every creature
    and the breath of all mankind. (Job 12:7–10)

When I spend time outside and notice all of the living plants and animals God sustains, I think about how he is truly in control. Right now in our area, millions of butterflies are migrating north from Mexico. How do they even know to do this? To me, they are just another reminder that God is in control. And when I think about how God is in control and I am not, this fact truly "restores my soul."

God's Presence

Our culture is now a couple of decades deep into the constant usage of technology, and we are all aware of what the research is revealing. Studies show that people are more lonely, anxious, and discontent than ever before.[2] Innately, we know even without concrete studies that being constantly stimulated and bombarded with information about other people leaves us with feelings of inadequacy and often despair. What if we were just . . . *still* sometimes?

Throughout the Bible are verses that guide us to "look up," "lift our eyes," and "see."

> I **lift up** my eyes to the mountains—
> 	where does my help come from? (Ps. 121:1)

> Taste and **see** that the LORD is good. (Ps. 34:8)

> **Lift up** your eyes and look to the heavens:
> 	Who created all these? (Isa. 40:26)

When we put our devices away and look at God's creation, we can lift our thoughts beyond other people, the problems in our lives, and the constant pressure to receive more information and be constantly available to the requests of others.

I think David was on the right track when he shared with us the power and serenity of spending time in God's beautiful outdoors. Let's get outside today to enjoy the flowers, the trees, the breeze, or the twinkling stars. When we do, I know this promise will ring true in our hearts:

> Surely your goodness and love will follow me
> 	all the days of my life,
> and I will dwell in the house of the LORD
> 	forever. (Ps. 23:6)

Key Ingredients

Denise

When Together

We show others we care dearly for them when we simply take the time to gather together and listen—really listen—while undistracted. A friend of mine, Jina, controls her phone. Her phone does not control her. When I am with Jina, her phone is nowhere in sight. There are no interruptions when we visit. I feel respected, special, and appreciated. She's listening to me, completely, and our relationship builds. It's like a breath of fresh air for me.

Yes, I know. This can't always be done. But the truth is, sometimes it *can* be done with a bit of effort and a few boundaries. We'll never be able to get rid of all our distractions and live in total peace, but with some careful planning and follow-through, our world can be transformed into something a little slower and more beautiful than its current cacophony of noise and distractions.

What are some ways you can unplug with others?

» Practice putting your devices away during mealtimes. Talk about it. Turn everything off and enjoy the people around you.

» Talk about God. Bring up a topic and see where it leads you. Prayer and Scripture at mealtimes are so meaningful, and fellowship fills the soul.

» Extend an invitation to a friend or loved one for a fun and simple picnic like ours or to take a walk. Perhaps start by saying, "I'm going to unplug for an hour and I'd love to take a walk with you. When are you free?"

» Take a nature walk with children. They find so many treasures along the way. Don't forget to bring a bag.

» Take a stroll in a city park with walking paths and fun playground equipment. If you're with children, swing alongside them if you're able. Talk to the person you're with about their day: the best, the worst, the easy, and the hard.

» Go for a beach walk, if you're near one, and dig for shells. Learn more about the area you live in with friends and loved ones.

» Invite a friend out to lunch. Keep your phone hidden and deliberately choose to listen with no interruptions.

» When at a meeting, church, and so forth, leave your phone in your car or another safe location.

» A scavenger hunt is a fun way to enjoy the backyard with all ages. Make it a competition if you can.

» Stargaze! We have a trampoline, so it's quite fun to fill it up with kids and adults alike. We check out the twinkly lights that God has not only created but named.

When Alone

Shh—the world can wait!

When I head out the door to take a walk on a nice day, the phone stays home, and I go it alone. I choose to walk into a space of just God and me and his beautiful dome of creation. I journey to the top of the hill way up on the ridge and straddle a gate overlooking miles of countryside. The cattle low with their calves close by. The meadowlark sings on a nearby fence post. And I sing too. The beauty of the earth overwhelms me, and I cannot help but sing praises to the Maker of the heavens and the earth.

What are some ways you can unplug?

» Take a long bubble bath. Silence the phone and place it in a location where you cannot hear it vibrate. Heavenly.

great things
can happen when you
unplug

» Purpose to look at your phone only at certain times of the day, if you can.

» Choose to multitask a little less. Watch some of the stress begin to diminish.

» Have your daily quiet time with the Lord, and make sure your devices are having a quiet time too.

Jenny shares: I once went on a class field trip with kindergartners to a nearby park. The kindergartners learned a lot of neat things about nature. The highlight of the kids' day was that they saw a baby deer (the highlight of my day, as well). I was reminded of the song "As the Deer" as I stared into the eyes of that spotted little creature. Just as the Bible says, we too thirst for God. He made us that way. We are most satisfied when we place Jesus Christ first in our lives and live for him.

Apron Application

1. As you go through your day, what distractions can you eliminate to have the greatest amount of quality in your relationships? In what ways can you be more fully present in your relationship with the Lord?

2. When we intentionally "unplug," what happens during this process? What do you notice? Ask God to help you become more aware of your distractions and set appropriate boundaries.

3. Make sure to carve out time for refreshment every day. How does this rejuvenate your soul?

Prayer

Heavenly Father, I come to you with thanksgiving and appreciation of the beauty you have created. Please help me to intentionally notice the green pastures and quiet waters you provide. I thank you for this healing in my soul. Lord, I want to love with all of me and not just some of me. Please give me the strength to set aside more intentional time with you and my relationships and to become more aware of my distractions. In Jesus's name, Amen.

Gather at Your Table

Our picnic was delightful because we spread out heirloom quilts under shade trees and made a relaxed setting for us to eat slowly and linger over conversation. Shelby had the idea to make an "unplugged" container, which encouraged everyone to place their cell phone aside during the meal. We specifically chose a flat, grassy area so the kids could play catch and we could all take in the beauty of the lake. As you'll see in the recipes that follow, we chose a light and refreshing menu that celebrated spring. To make sure the recipes were easy to eat outside on the go, we intentionally used fun containers such as wooden berry baskets, small Mason jars, and waffle bowls.

Strawberry Lemonade

Prep time: 10 minutes
Yield: 4 (12–16 oz.) servings

1½ cups fresh lemon juice (about 5–6 lemons), divided
1½ cups strawberries, trimmed and halved
1 cup sugar
4 cups cold water

Directions

1. Juice lemons into a measuring cup, keeping as many seeds out as possible.
2. Puree strawberries with 2 Tbs lemon juice in a blender until smooth, then use a wooden spoon to force mixture through a fine sieve into a bowl to remove seeds.
3. Mix together puree, remaining lemon juice, sugar, and water in a large pitcher until sugar is dissolved.
4. Taste and add more sugar or water to desired flavor. Serve over ice.

   Can be prepared ahead of time and stored in a refrigerated, airtight pitcher for up to three days.

Cucumber Dip

Prep time: 10–15 minutes
Yield: 8 servings

3 large cucumbers, seeded and diced
1 tomato, diced
1 bell pepper, diced
1–2 bunches green onions, thinly sliced on the diagonal (or sub 1 tsp onion salt)
2 cups cheddar or Colby jack cheese, shredded
¾ cup green goddess salad dressing
½ tsp garlic salt or garlic powder
salt and pepper to taste

Directions

1. In a large mixing bowl, combine all ingredients well and chill until serving.
2. Serve with tortilla chips or pita chips, or alone as a salad.

Tortellini Pasta Salad

Prep time: 25 minutes
Cook time: 15 minutes
Yield: 10–12 servings

For the salad

2 cups	fresh snow peas
2 cups	broccoli florets
2 cups	button mushrooms, sliced
2½ cups	cherry tomatoes, halved
1 (6 oz.) can	black olives, drained
8 oz.	cheese-stuffed tortellini
3 oz.	fettuccine, uncooked
1 Tbs	Parmesan cheese, grated

For the dressing

½ cup	green onions, sliced
⅓ cup	red wine vinegar
⅓ cup	olive oil
2 Tbs	fresh parsley, chopped
2 cloves	garlic, minced
2 tsp	dried basil
1 tsp	dried dill weed
1 tsp	salt
½ tsp	pepper
½ tsp	sugar
½ tsp	dried oregano
1½ tsp	Dijon mustard

Directions

1. In a large pot, boil snow peas and broccoli for one minute. Drain and let cool. When at room temperature, combine peas and broccoli with mushrooms, tomatoes, and olives in a large bowl.
2. Cook tortellini and fettucine according to package directions. Drain and cool.
3. Combine cooled pasta with vegetables.
4. Mix together all ingredients for dressing. Shake well in a tightly covered jar (a pint jar works well for this) or other container. Pour over tortellini and vegetables and toss well.
5. Chill several hours before serving. Garnish with Parmesan cheese.

Roast Beef Spread

4 cups roast beef, sliced and roughly chopped
2 Tbs dill pickle relish or coarsely chopped fresh dill pickles
dash garlic powder
½ cup mayonnaise (plus more, if desired)

Directions

Mix all ingredients together and spread on crackers, buns, or hard rolls.

Note: This is a great way to use up leftover roast beef.

Fresh Fruit with Almond Sugar
in a Waffle Bowl

1 pint strawberries, trimmed and halved
1 pineapple, peeled, cored, and cut into bite-sized chunks
2 peaches, sliced
1 pint blueberries
1 cup green grapes
1 cup red grapes
1 tsp almond extract
1 Tbs sugar or sugar substitute
12 waffle bowls (in the ice cream cone section)
fresh mint leaves for garnish

Directions

1. Mix all fruit together. Stir in the almond extract and sugar.
2. Spoon into waffle bowls and garnish with a fresh mint leaf.

Annie shares: The almond extract in this recipe is the "secret ingredient" that my mom has been adding to her fruit salads for years. You won't believe how distinctively delicious it makes the fruit taste!

Strawberry Shortcake

4–6 cups	fresh or frozen strawberries, sliced
⅓ cup	sugar, divided
2 cups	all-purpose flour
1 Tbs	baking powder
½ tsp	salt
½ cup	cold butter or margarine, cubed (1 stick)
1	egg, beaten
⅔ cup	whole milk or whipping cream
2 cups	homemade whipped cream or whipped topping

Prep time: 15 minutes
Cook time: 12 minutes
Yield: 8 servings

Directions

1. Preheat oven to 450°.
2. Combine strawberries and 2 Tbs sugar in a large bowl; stir and set aside.
3. Stir flour, baking powder, and salt together in a large mixing bowl; cut in butter with a fork or pastry blender.
4. Whisk egg and milk together in a small bowl; add to dry mixture, stirring until well blended and moistened.
5. Separate the dough in half and spread in two greased, 8-inch round baking pans. (It's helpful to flour your hands first, as the dough is sticky and a bit difficult to work with.) Build edges up slightly. Wet your hand and shake water droplets lightly on top of dough. Sprinkle with remaining sugar.
6. Bake for 12–15 minutes, until slightly browned. Remove from pans and cool on racks.
7. Once cooled, top with strawberries and whipped cream and serve.

Individual Mason jar directions

With a biscuit cutter, cut out two shortcake rounds for each Mason jar. Layer it how you wish, ending with a dollop of whipped cream and a few strawberry slices on each.

Prep time: 20 minutes
Cook time: 12 minutes
Yield: 8 individual jars

33

Ladies' Brunch

Nourishing Both Body & Soul

Cucumber Lemon Water

Sunrise Berry Spritzer

Mini Egg Frittatas

German Bundt Cake (Poppy Seed Cake)

Blueberry Scones with Glaze

Frozen Fruit Cups

The spring months are some of the busiest on the farm. All of our guys spend every waking minute with one goal in mind: to get the planting of soybeans and corn finished! Because of their long work hours, we ladies can begin to feel a little lonely.

So when we met together to plan our year of gatherings, we kept in mind that in the spring we often feel a bit depleted. We talked about how we could create a gathering that was particularly feminine and fun but that would also feed our souls. The idea of the "lonely ladies' brunch" was hatched, and we looked forward to it with great anticipation. We planned a meal that included simple yet elegant and delightfully girly dishes. Mom suggested using my grandma's real china dishes to bring some joy into a challenging season. Keeping our spiritual nourishment in mind, we decided this was the perfect opportunity to be refreshed by storing up God's Word in our hearts. We planned which recipes to make and we also planned to read Titus 2 together for the event; we would come prepared to discuss this passage about what it means to truly be a godly woman.

I once read that Corrie ten Boom, a famous Christian Holocaust rescuer, came from a family who believed that not only one's body but also one's spirit should be nourished during every meal. Her family practiced reading whole chapters of God's Word and discussing it together before they took their first bite of each meal. Because of this strong spiritual nourishment, she and the other members of her family turned out to be world changers! The story of the ten Boom family's practice confirms the power of God's Word to strengthen, guide, and nourish. I think of the promises of Psalm 19:7–10, which lists the benefits of God's Word: refreshment, righteousness, joy, wisdom . . . more valuable than gold. This passage compels us to absorb more of God's Word into our lives in whatever ways we can.

When we arrived at Shelby's house, we saw that she'd beautifully set the dining room table with Grandma Betty's white and silver china, silver candlesticks, and light pink peonies. Shelby had thoughtfully prepared a Sunrise Berry

Spritzer for each of us in dainty stemmed glasses. As we each brought in the dishes we had prepared, we saw family favorites such as Blueberry Scones with Glaze, frosty Frozen Fruit Cups, and Mini Egg Frittatas—all for us to savor with each other.

We sat down together, oohing and ahhing over the sophisticated table and feeling pampered. We began our time with prayer, praying over our busy families and asking God to sustain us during a demanding season. And then we thoroughly enjoyed our meal, eating slowly and delighting in the sweet and savory dishes. The candlelit room and the beautiful flowers set the scene perfectly to relax and enjoy.

My favorite part of this event was the biblical discussion we shared as women. Mom had a few questions prepared to help us really dig deep into Titus 2, especially verses 4 and 5:

> And so train the young women to love their husbands and children, to be self-controlled, pure, working at home, kind, and submissive to their own husbands, that the word of God may not be reviled. (ESV)

She also shared her perspective as an older woman in Christ, and we girls talked about our roles as younger women who greatly desire to please our Lord. How can we be kind in a hurried, frazzled world? What does it look like to be pure and self-controlled? How can we guard against reviling the Word of God by obeying his commands for us?

I'm so thankful that I am part of a family who encourages me to strive to be this kind of woman. I love that we can delve into God's Word to find strength and nourishment and build ourselves up to go out in the world with purpose. I left the ladies' brunch feeling not one bit lonely but instead nourished—both physically and spiritually.

A Place at His Table

Shelby

It is important to know God's Word and allow it to nourish us. God's Word is truth, his Word is powerful, and his Word is living. When we learn and follow God's Scriptures, we give it the power to transform our lives.

Psalm 119, the longest chapter of the Bible, has a theme of confessing the greatness and truth of God's Word. It is all-sufficient and all-encompassing.

> *I have hidden your word in my heart*
> *that I might not sin against you. (v. 11)*

When we read and understand Scripture, we can easily recollect it in times of need and utilize it in all areas of life, especially as a way to curb us from sin. We must follow God's Word and let it guide us by seeking and applying it to our lives.

> *You are my refuge and my shield;*
> *I have put my hope in your word. (v. 114)*

When we are growing in God's Word and place our hope in what it says, then we know and believe God *is* our strength and help.

> *My soul is weary with sorrow;*
> *strengthen me according to your word. (v. 28)*

Scripture can help guide us through our hard times. God assures us that in our sorrow there will be beacons of hope to help us navigate the darkness. If we can hold tight to his Word and the promises he speaks, we can remain strong and gain strength in knowing God is never changing and will lead us through. If we focus on God daily, he can bring the healing we need with time.

Your word is a lamp to my feet
and a light to my path. (v. 105 ESV)

Throughout my walk as a Christian, I have found that it's easier to be in relationship with the Lord when I am in his Word. There's great power and strength in Scripture in times of worry, in lending forgiveness, and even in happiness. I challenge you to allow God's Word to infiltrate you and be pivotal in your life as well. Work hard to embed his truth in your heart.

Key Ingredients

Denise

Do you see yourself having your own ladies' brunch? What does that look like in your mind's eye? What can you imagine in your own home? Who would be your guests to nourish mind, soul, and body? Or maybe your home doesn't work but a quaint restaurant does.

Recently our church's women's ministry team decided to do this very thing! We organized four get-togethers, calling them "Conversations around the Table." Our intention was to gather women together in a comfortable home setting. We would eat something easy but delicious, hear a beautiful testimony of how the Lord transformed a life, listen to a lesson, and then implement the spiritual content into questions during our conversation time around the table. Through these gatherings, we made new friends and built stronger relationships with those we already knew. This is a picture of sharing our faith in Jesus and "encouraging one another, and all the more as [we] see the Day drawing near" (Heb. 10:25 ESV).

Women are created for detailed relationships and love to be pampered. It's not very often we take time out of our busy lives for these indulgences. But we must take the time to gather, "For where two or three gather in my name, there am I with them" (Matt. 18:20).

We Gingham Apron girls made a plan to meet our needs physically, emotionally, and spiritually at this gathering. We were hungry for all three components, and we took action. How about you? Here are some ideas:

» Start with a dream. What would you desire to do with friends? Get together and come up with a plan. Anticipation is a key ingredient. Enjoy the process!

» Set a spiritual theme. Perhaps you'd like to talk about parenting or marriage? Maybe stewardship or the fruit of the Spirit or the struggles you have been dealing with? This intentionally sets the tone for a lot of the conversation.

» Will you set a theme for the meal? Maybe Italian or a garden party? Color schemes and florals? Getting everyone involved in brainstorming helps us learn more about each other—our likes and dislikes.

» Menu planning is fun. Let everyone have a say in it to take ownership. Perhaps you would prefer a nice restaurant rather than hosting? That's okay.

» If you choose to host, remember your focus is on fellowship, not on having a perfectly spick-and-span house.

» Have a virtual party through FaceTime, Zoom, or Skype if your loved ones are not physically near.

Apron Application

Molly

1. How can you practice storing up God's Word in your heart (Prov. 2:1)? Find a particular book of the Bible you're interested in, or follow along with the Sunday sermon at your local church as a starting point. Psalms or Proverbs can be good beginning places as well.

2. Who can you reach out to this week? Someone may just be waiting for that invitation. Prayerfully consider those who could use refreshment.

3. In your relationships, what can you share about how God is working in your life? Friendships grow and prosper when we are transparent and can share the depths of our lives with one another.

Prayer

Heavenly Father, thank you so much for your powerful, sustaining Word. Let us not forget the importance of taking the time to understand the depths of your teaching and dwell on it in our hearts. Lord, we are called to gather together and to find refreshment for our body and spirit. Please help us intentionally seek out others in our lives to be fulfilled through nourishment, your unchanging truth, and relationships with one another. In Jesus's name, Amen.

Gather at Your Table

The candles, fresh flowers, and white and silver china added a simple elegance to this meal that made it memorable, and the neutral color palette lent a restful and refreshing atmosphere. Even if you don't have china or stemmed glasses in your cabinet, you can still achieve this look with decorated paper plates and cups. We specifically chose simple foods that could be prepared in advance because this occasion fell during a very busy season, and the last thing we wanted was to add stress with fussy recipes. When planning a gathering like this, make anything you can prepare days or weeks in advance, and don't hesitate to grab something from a local bakery.

Cucumber Lemon Water

   1   lemon, seeded and thinly sliced
  ½   cucumber, seeded and thinly sliced
  8 cups   cold water

Prep time: 5 minutes
  + 1 hour (or longer)
  chill time
Yield: 8 (8 oz.) servings

Directions

1. Add sliced lemon and cucumber slices to bottom of a pitcher. Use a wooden spoon to lightly muddle several times to release juices and flavor.
2. Add water and stir.
3. Cover and refrigerate from 1 to 24 hours.

   Note: If by accident you did not get all of the seeds removed earlier, they may float to the top; if so, spoon out floating seeds before serving. Enjoy.

Sunrise Berry Spritzer

  ½ gal.   orange juice, preferably pulp-free
  1½ cups   pineapple juice
  1 Tbs   lemon juice
  24 oz.   lemon-lime soda
  8 oz.   frozen sliced strawberries
           ice

Prep time: 5 minutes
  + 30 minutes (or longer)
  chill time
Yield: 18 (6 oz.) servings

Directions

1. In a big glass pitcher, mix together orange juice, pineapple juice, lemon juice, and soda.
2. Add frozen sliced strawberries and mix together. Chill for at least 30 minutes, until ready to serve.
3. Pour over ice and enjoy. Garnish with orange and/or strawberry slices, if desired.

Mini Egg Frittatas

Prep time: 20 minutes
Cook time: 15 minutes
Yield: 12 servings

3 Tbs	olive oil, divided
2	small baking potatoes, peeled and diced (approx. 1½ cups)
½ cup	chopped sweet pepper
10 oz.	breakfast sausage
1 cup	fresh spinach
4	large eggs
¼ cup	milk
¼ cup	Parmesan cheese, grated
	salt and pepper, to taste

Directions

1. Preheat oven to 375°.
2. Line a 12-cup muffin pan with paper liners.
3. In a large frying pan over medium heat, warm 2 Tbs olive oil. Add the potatoes and peppers. Sauté until they begin to soften, about 5 minutes. Crumble in the sausage and cook, stirring often, until golden brown. Remove from heat and transfer to a bowl to cool. Gently wipe out the pan with a paper towel. Heat the remaining 1 Tbs olive oil and add spinach. Sauté until dark green and wilted, approximately 1–2 minutes. Add to potatoes and sausage.
4. In a bowl, whisk together eggs, milk, and cheese until blended. Stir in the cooled sausage and potato mixture.
5. Scoop the mixture into lined muffin cups, dividing evenly and filling about ¾ full.
6. Bake until firm and doubled in size, 10–15 minutes. Let cool slightly in the pan before serving.

German Bundt Cake

(Poppy Seed Cake)

Prep time: 10 minutes
Cook time: 45–50 minutes
Yield: 10 servings

⅓ cup	poppy seeds
	warm water
1 pkg.	white cake mix
½ cup	vegetable oil
1 (3.4 oz.) pkg.	instant vanilla pudding mix
4	eggs

For the icing

1 cup	powdered sugar
2 Tbs	butter, melted
1 tsp	vanilla
1–2 Tbs	warm water

Directions

1. Preheat oven to 350°. Grease a Bundt or angel food cake pan well. Set aside.
2. In a liquid measuring cup, add the poppy seeds, then fill with enough warm water to reach 1 cup.
3. In a large mixing bowl, combine cake mix, oil, and poppy seed/water mixture.
4. Mix in eggs one at a time. Beat until fully blended.
5. Pour batter into prepared pan and bake for 45–50 minutes, or until a toothpick comes out clean.
6. Let cool slightly, then place a sheet of waxed paper on counter. Place a wire rack on top of Bundt pan and carefully invert pan, then place rack on waxed paper. Remove pan, then sprinkle cake with desired amount of powdered sugar while still warm. Or, if desired, cool completely and frost with icing.
7. To make the icing, stir all ingredients together until smooth and somewhat runny. Drizzle over cake.

Blueberry Scones with Glaze

Prep time: 10 minutes
Cook time: 20–25 minutes
Yield: 8 servings

For the scones

2 cups	all-purpose flour
½ cup	sugar
2½ tsp	baking powder
½ tsp	ground cinnamon
½ tsp	salt
½ cup	cold butter (1 stick)
½ cup	milk
1	egg
½ tsp	lemon juice
1 tsp	vanilla extract
1 heaping cup	blueberries (fresh or frozen; do not thaw if frozen)
	sugar for sprinkling on top before baking

For the glaze

1 cup	powdered sugar
3 Tbs	milk
¼ tsp	vanilla

Directions

1. Preheat oven to 400°. Line a large baking sheet with parchment paper. Set aside.
2. In a large bowl, whisk together flour, sugar, baking powder, cinnamon, and salt.
3. Grate butter and toss into the flour mixture; cut in with a fork or pastry blender until mixture resembles coarse meal. Set aside.
4. In a small bowl, whisk together milk, egg, lemon juice, and vanilla. Stir into the flour mixture until moistened. Fold in blueberries carefully. Do not overwork the dough. It will be a little wet. With floured hands, work the dough into a ball as best you can and transfer to prepared baking sheet.
5. Press into a neat 8-inch disc and cut into 8 equal wedges with a pizza cutter. Separate the pieces from each other, leaving about ½ inch between each piece. Top with a sprinkle of sugar.
6. Bake for 20–25 minutes or until lightly golden. Remove from the oven and allow to cool for a few minutes.
7. To make the glaze, whisk all of the glaze ingredients together and drizzle lightly over scones right before serving.

Frozen Fruit Cups

Prep time: 30 minutes
Yield: 24 servings

4 cups	sugar
8 cups	very warm water
1 can	pineapple tidbits, any size
1 jar	maraschino cherries, any size, undrained
1 can	mandarin oranges, any size, undrained
1 (12 oz.) can	frozen lemonade concentrate
1 (12 oz.) can	frozen orange juice concentrate

Optional add-ins

4–6	peaches, peeled, pitted, and chopped
1 qt.	sliced or chopped strawberries
1 pt.	blueberries
2–3	sliced bananas

(This recipes varies a lot depending on what fruits are in season.)

1 pkg.	plastic punch cups, approximately 24 (6–8 oz.)

Directions

1. Pour sugar and water into a very large bowl; stir to dissolve sugar.
2. Combine desired fruits with juice concentrates and sugar/water mixture until well blended.
3. Fill plastic cups with fruit and juice mixture. Place in freezer on cookie sheets until frozen.

Jenny shares: A friend at church shared this recipe with me. I enjoy these fruit cups most in the summer because they are so refreshing and are cool and tasty on a hot day. These are perfect for the whole family.

Tea Party

*Considering Others
Better Than Yourself*

Raspberry Lemon Water

Fresh Fruit Kabobs with Strawberry Dip

Pimento-Crab Sandwiches

Cucumber Sandwiches

Chocolate Caramel Pecan Bars

Bacon & Tomato Finger Sandwiches

Almond & Raspberry Finger Sandwiches

Petits Fours

Napoleons

We'd had a busy day full of housework, tumbling, violin and guitar lessons, and all of the other busyness that comes with a home full of energetic children. At 3:30, I told my girls to put on last year's Easter dresses and fix their hair because it was time to go to a tea party at Grandma's!

When we arrived, it was like a breath of fresh air after a long and weary day. Mom, wearing her signature apron, greeted each of us at the kitchen door with a big hug and smile. My little boys were greeted by my dad. Having no interest in a girly tea party, they quickly put on boots and work gloves and eagerly joined Grandpa for chores.

We entered the kitchen to find more of our favorite people—Aunt Shelby, Aunt Jenny, Aunt Molly, and of course the girl cousins, Anna and Ava. All of these ladies were in their pretty summer clothes too.

We walked out to the backyard shelter to find a table beautifully laid with fine china, spring flowers, and several very special, dainty dishes. Mom had worked hard, taking time out of her busy schedule to make a lovely special event. She reflected Philippians 2:3–4 to us: "In humility value others above yourselves, [looking] to the interests of the others."

What a refreshing and fun treat it was to be at this tea party. As we ate, we had warm conversation. We reminisced about the tea party we'd had a few years back when the royal wedding of Prince William and Princess Kate took place. We shared memories about how our special Grandma Betty, who had English roots, had been with us and how much she'd enjoyed our enthusiasm for the special event.

My mom had asked each of us to bring a teacup and saucer special to us, and during our meal we each took a bit of time to tell about our cup and saucer and the dear person who had given it to us. I learned a lot about Shelby's and Molly's grandmothers, and I reminisced about my grandmothers as well. What a fun way to bring our unique heritages into this gathering!

Throughout the meal we also discussed table manners with our girls, emphasizing that they are a good way to show love and respect for others and are

another way to consider others better than ourselves. We ended up playing a manners game, which was a fun way to practice with the little ladies.

This tea party at my mom's made me think about the many tea parties I've attended through the years. I had lots of such "parties" with both of my grandmothers, and they were so special while completely different. When I'd visit my proper Grandma Betty, we'd have tea in fine china cups with saucers and sit at a table covered with a lace tablecloth she had made herself. Of course she always had a special homemade treat prepared too. But I also remember having little parties with my Grandma Maxine. I can't refer to them as parties, because we never had tea! But Grandma Maxine laid out a spread that I absolutely loved. Her specialties were "mousie sandwiches," composed of a tiny piece of Velveeta smashed between two oyster crackers, "skunk cookies," those packaged cookies that are chocolate on the back and striped on the front, and a jug of "orange drink." We'd talk, and I'd get her laughing so hard she couldn't stop. Sometimes we'd sing together, and I remember her singing "The Old Rugged Cross." It was during one of these special visits that she told me all about being saved as a teenage girl.

I have since realized that all of these parties, from proper English teas to spreads of grocery store goodies, were times when women in my life considered others better than themselves—beautiful reflections of Philippians 2:3. In their own unique ways, whether fancy or plain, women can show love to others by gathering around a table, serving something delicious to eat and drink, and engaging in meaningful conversation.

A Place at His Table

Shelby —————

Considering others better than ourselves can come in many different forms. Annie shared a great comparison between the two different styles of tea (or "not tea") parties both of her grandmas hosted. Despite the differences, there was one common theme: godly women humbly serving their granddaughters.

Can you think of the last time you considered someone better than yourself? How about looking past your own interest to that of others? Think beyond your children, spouse, or somebody else of great significance to you. Those are the people in our lives who are generally easier to serve because we love them deeply. But what about the individuals whom you feel may have more superior talents than you or whom you are certain just try to get under your skin? How about the people who have fewer accomplishments and less experience, or maybe belong to a different political party than you? When was the last time you looked to their interests over your own?

When Jesus was here on earth, he didn't look only to his own interests or only to the interests of those who were likeminded, who had a similar educational background, or who shared his economic class. He spent time with those who needed him, those who were seeking what he offered, those who wanted to bless him. He also spent time with those who dismissed that he was the Son of God and those who were difficult and looking for controversy. When it came to other people, Jesus displayed an attitude of humility and considered others better than himself. He handled people with grace, courage, love, and kindness.

In this life it's easy to find ourselves falling into the traps of selfishness, jealousy, or prejudice; we live in a fallen world. When I start going down that destructive path, I quickly realize I am not walking in my faith as I should be.

These times are a good reminder to turn my focus back to the Lord, dig into God's Word more, pray more, and shift my attention off of myself and onto God and what I am called to do. When our love for God is stronger than our love for ourselves, we gain a more accurate perception—of ourselves and of others. It is then we realize that we are *all* sinners, *all* made by God, and *all* valuable to God.

When we are confident in our own identity in Christ, it's easier to steer away from the pitfalls of selfish ambition and extend grace and love to those around us.

> *Do not think of yourself more highly than you ought, but rather think of yourself with sober judgment, in accordance with the faith God has distributed to each of you. (Rom. 12:3)*

Genuine humility and sincere interest in others incite personal growth and also build up our families, churches, and communities. What can you do today to consider others better than yourself and look to their interests?

Key Ingredients

Gathering around a "tea party" table of beauty fascinates me. I delight in the intricate details of the specialty foods. Beautiful dishes (one of my many weaknesses) often reflect a history I must discover. The ambiance of lighted candles pulls me in. The linens—were these handed down? Grandma's? Great-grandma's? Everything about a well-planned stage is truly delicious to my romantic soul.

This "fluff" is the bait that gently ties us all together before we move to concentrating on each other as individuals. We choose to say, "How are you?" "What's going on in your life?" "What have you been up to lately?" My favorite author, Anne Ortlund, writes, "There are two kinds of personalities in this world, and you are one of the two. People can tell which, as soon as you walk into a room: your attitude says either 'Here I am,' or 'There you are.'"[1] Oh, how I want to be a "there you are" person. It truly sets the stage for considering others above ourselves.

I have a secret. Even though I am an outgoing person, I find it hard to be vulnerable and authentic beyond the comfort zone of my family. Perhaps it's that feeling of inadequacy in many areas of my life. *Will they judge me? Will they really like me as a friend if I truly reveal myself?* Then I defend my scary feelings and ask myself, *Why should I even care what they think?* But I do. We all do. I want them to like me. I want the friendship. I want them to truly care about *me*. I think Satan tries to keep us a bit intimidated so that we will not go beyond our comfortable boundaries. And yet I know that when someone bares her soul to me, I respect and appreciate her courage and honesty so much. From this, a deepening of our relationship occurs.

We *need* each other. Look and listen to discern the needs of others. Laugh with, cry with, understand and feel empathy for, and celebrate and shout and belly-laugh with others. Talk about what the Lord has done and pray others will see the Lord in your life.

Hosting a fancy gathering is so much fun, and others love it too. Do you want to host a fancier type of gathering, like one of our tea parties? Consider some of these ideas as a head start.

Make It a Special Event

Create a menu. Look up some fancy appetizers, dainty sandwiches, and pretty desserts. Create a menu that will make eyes pop. Lessen the load by delegating some of the food items and other tasks. Believe it or not, this brings

Menu

Drinks

Raspberry Lemon Water
Hot Tea

Fresh fruit kabobs with
    Strawberry cream cheese dip
Bacon Tomato Sandwiches
Pimento Cheese Sandwiches
Cucumber Sandwiches
Almond butter and raspberry
    jam Sandwiches

Desserts

Chocolate Caramel Pecan Bars
Chocolate Napoleans
Cream Puffs
Petit Fours

responsibility and a bit of ownership to the guests in a way they may appreciate, making them feel a little closer to the group. It also gives each guest something more to discuss.

Dress for the occasion. Don an outfit that makes you feel your best. Fix your hair. Wear gloves and a hat if you'd like.

Bring out the good dishes. Many of us have a few good dishes sitting around in cabinets we don't open often. They're sitting there patiently, just waiting to be put to use. And, yes, silverware, fancy tablecloths, and cloth napkins too. If you don't have them, perhaps you could buy some decorative paper plates, cups, and napkins. Making the extra effort is worth it!

Set the ambiance. Add some background music and lighted candles.

Send out invitations. Receiving an invitation in the mail makes me smile. You can do that for others too. And while you're working with paper and ink, create a name card for each place setting too.

Create Teachable Moments

Learn manners the fun way. Gatherings like this can be the perfect time to teach some simple etiquette to yourself and to younger generations. You can make a game of it at the event, as Annie mentioned earlier, or you can practice some etiquette before coming—or both. "May I be excused?" "Which way *do* I pass the plates?"

Engage with conversation starters. The hostess can prepare some conversation starters in advance and place them at each table setting. Through good etiquette, we can encourage good conversational skills.

Consider including spiritual aspects. Be a good listener. Ask questions. This can be a good time for thoughtful prayer and devotions. How about asking guests to read a short biography of a well-known Christian like Elisabeth Elliott and then planning a time for discussion? Or sing a hymn together or ask each person to quote a Bible verse. There are so many ways to invite the Lord to partake with you.

Apron Application

Molly

1. What woman or girl in your life can you write a handwritten note to and praise in some way?

2. How can you practice humility throughout your week by using good manners and/or affirmations? Why is this important? In what areas of your life do you find yourself slipping?

3. In what ways have others' gestures of kindness made you feel treasured? Consider how you can be more intentional about doing this for others.

Prayer

Heavenly Father, I am so thankful to share in this calling of being a woman, and I delight in fellowship with other women. Please help us consider others better than ourselves by taking the time to invite, welcome in, and offer undivided attention. Rid my heart of any selfishness, so that I can put others above myself in all areas of my life. Thank you, Father, for giving us the gifts of warm, comforting drinks and an endless variety of delicious foods that satisfy and delight us. Please help us look to you for our true beauty and be reminded that we are worth far more than rubies. In Jesus's name I pray, Amen.

Gather at Your Table

The tea party was packed full of feminine fun. Each place was set with a different china pattern, bringing warm, touching memories of cherished grandmothers and aunts who once owned the special dishes. The recipes we prepared for this gathering were delicately small and pretty, and could easily include cream puffs or other fun store-bought dainties as well. And the manners game provided a lighthearted activity that really drew in the young girls.

Raspberry Lemon Water

Prep time: 5 minutes
+ chill time
Yield: 8 (8 oz.) servings

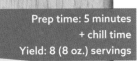

2 qts. water
1 cup fresh raspberries
4 lemon slices, seeds removed

Directions

1. Combine all ingredients in a large glass pitcher.
2. Cover and refrigerate 12–24 hours.
3. Strain before serving.

Fresh Fruit Kabobs
with Strawberry Dip

Prep time: 20 minutes
Yield: 2–3 skewers
per guest

For the skewers*

fresh pineapple, cut into small pieces
fresh strawberries, cut into quarters
fresh red grapes, whole
fresh peaches, cut into small pieces
fresh blueberries, whole

*Any colorful, good-for-dipping fruit may be used, as long as you end up with about 5 cups total. Be sure to choose fruit that's in season.

For the dip

½ (13.5 oz.) pkg. strawberry glaze (in the produce section next to strawberries)
6 oz. strawberry yogurt
1 cup whipped topping

Directions

1. Arrange fruit skewers as desired and place on a large tray or baking sheet. Plan for 2 to 3 skewers for each guest.
2. In a bowl, mix together glaze and yogurt.
3. Fold in whipped topping. This makes a bright pink dip.
   Place the bowl of fruit dip in the center of the tray.

Pimento-Crab Sandwiches

6 slices	soft white bread
1 jar	pimento cheese spread
1 (6 oz.) can	crabmeat
2 Tbs	mayonnaise
dash	onion powder
	salt and pepper, to taste

optional: garnish with celery, parsley, or cilantro leaves

Prep time: 10 minutes
Yield: 24 small sandwiches

Directions

1. Stack bread and cut off crusts with bread knife. Spread pimento spread on 3 slices.
2. In a bowl, mix the remaining ingredients. Add more mayonnaise if needed.
3. Spread remaining 3 slices of bread generously with crab filling.
4. Put the slices together to make 3 sandwiches. Cut in half, then halve again to make 4 small rectangles per sandwich. Garnish as desired.

Cucumber Sandwiches

1 loaf	presliced pumpernickel or rye bread
8 oz.	cream cheese, softened
½ tsp	garlic powder
¼ tsp	onion powder
	salt and pepper, to taste
1	cucumber, peeled and sliced
	dill weed for garnish

Prep time: 10 minutes
Yield: 24 sandwiches

Directions

1. Mix together cream cheese, garlic powder, onion powder, and salt and pepper.
2. Spread cream cheese mixture on 24 pumpernickel bread slices. Place one cucumber slice on each bread slice.
3. Garnish with dill weed.

Chocolate Caramel Pecan Bars

Prep time: 15 minutes
Cook time: 25 minutes
Yield: 18 squares

1 cup   all-purpose flour
1 cup   rolled oats
¾ cup   brown sugar
½ tsp   baking soda
¼ tsp   salt
¾ cup   butter, melted
32   individually wrapped caramels (or 11 oz. bag baking caramel melts)
⅓ cup   evaporated milk
½ tsp   butter flavoring
1 cup   milk chocolate chips
1 cup   pecans, chopped

Directions

1. Preheat oven to 350°.
2. Combine first six ingredients and mix well.
3. Press into the bottom of a 9x13 pan.
4. Bake for 10 minutes.
5. In a small saucepan, combine caramels, evaporated milk, and butter flavoring and melt over medium-low heat, stirring regularly, until fully melted and creamy. Do not boil.
6. Pour over baked crust and spread evenly, then sprinkle top with chocolate chips and pecans.
7. Bake for an additional 15 minutes. Let cool before slicing.

Shelby shares: This recipe came from my Aunt Linda and is one of my favorite rich desserts. When each of my three children were born, my aunt would come to visit and graciously deliver a gift for the baby—and a pan of these bars for me.

— Bacon & Tomato Finger Sandwiches —

Prep time: 10 minutes
Yield: 18 tea sandwiches

18 small tea sandwich–size slices of good white bread (we prefer to bake a frozen Rhodes bread loaf in a shaped bread tube)

4 Roma tomatoes, sliced thin

For sandwich spread

¼ cup mayonnaise
¼ cup sour cream
2 Tbs crumbled bacon
½ tsp onion powder
¼ tsp garlic powder
¼ tsp salt

Directions

1. Cut white bread into tea-size slices, if not presliced.
2. Combine all spread ingredients and mix well. Spread evenly on each slice of bread.
3. Top each piece with sliced tomato.
4. If desired, sprinkle with fresh-cracked pepper.

— Almond & Raspberry Finger Sandwiches —

Prep time: 30 minutes
Yield: 8–10 finger
     sandwiches, depending
     on the size of cookie
     cutter

1 loaf country-style bread, sliced
1 (15 oz.) jar almond butter
1 (15 oz.) jar black or red raspberry jelly

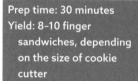

Directions

1. Using a cookie cutter of your choice, cut a shape from each slice of bread (I used a flower shape). (You can get two shapes from each slice if cutter is small enough.)
2. Using a second, very small cutter, cut a shape in the center of half of the pieces so the jelly will show through. (These will be the tops.)
3. On whole pieces (the bottom slices), spread almond butter. Dollop a little jelly in the middle.
4. Place the top pieces and line up the edges neatly.
5. Place in an airtight container until ready to serve.

Petits Fours

Prep time: 45 minutes
Cook time: 20 minutes
Yield: approx. 2 dozen

1 box   yellow or white cake mix

For the icing

9 cups   powdered sugar
½ cup   corn syrup
½ cup   water
1 tsp   almond flavoring
         food coloring, if desired

Directions

1. Preheat oven and prepare cake mix according to box directions. Bake in a jelly roll pan (approx. 10x15). Cool completely.
2. Use cookie cutters to cut out different designs or slice into small squares or diamonds, and place cake pieces on a wire rack set over a bowl or pan (I use a small cookie sheet).
3. Mix powdered sugar, corn syrup, water, and flavoring in top pan of double boiler over simmering water. Heat until icing is very warm and runny. At this point you can divide and make different colors, if desired. Work quickly. If icing becomes thick, place pan back over double boiler to thin out.
4. Pour warm icing over cooled cakes. Reuse the overflow icing if needed.
5. Decorate to your liking with flowers, frosting flowers, or purchased cake decorations.

Napoleons

1 box	frozen puff pastry
2 cups	homemade whipped cream or whipped topping, divided
1 (3.9 oz.) box	instant chocolate pudding mix, prepared according to directions
½ cup	semisweet chocolate chips

Prep time: 45 minutes
Cook time: 15 minutes
Yield: approx. 2 dozen

Directions

1. Thaw pastry according to package directions; roll out and cut into shapes of your liking. (We've used cookie cutters or cut in ½ by 1-inch rectangles.)
2. Bake pastry according to package directions. Cool completely. Each will be puffed up. Split horizontally to make bottoms and tops.
3. Fold 1 cup whipped cream into 1 cup pudding until well combined.
4. Fill each bottom pastry half with about 1 tsp chocolate/cream mixture. Place pastry tops.
5. Pipe or dollop a small amount of whipped cream or whipped topping onto each top.
6. Microwave the chocolate chips in 20-second intervals, stirring each time, until melted. Pipe or drizzle a fine stream of chocolate on top of each pastry.
7. Refrigerate immediately for at least 30 minutes or until ready to serve.

   Note: Napoleons can be made in advance and refrigerated 24–48 hours before serving.

Summer

Favorite Pie Party

Showing the Love of Christ through Simple Hospitality

Simple Pie Crust

Coconut Cream Pie

Banana Cream Pie

French Chocolate Pie

Grandma Betty's (Easiest Ever) Key Lime Pie

Cherry Pie

Fresh Peach Blueberry Pie

Strawberry Cream Cheese Slab Pie

In Iowa, summer is breathtaking. We're surrounded by lush green crops growing and in full bloom by July. Sweet corn stands and farmers' markets are open, ripe, red tomatoes dangle from their plants, our highway ditches are filled with wildflowers, and the light blue chicory and Queen Anne's lace look like they came right out of a fairy tale. We hear frogs bellowing from the pond nearby and an occasional meadowlark singing its melody.

Summer to me is a season of freedom, simple living, and embracing all the activities the time of year has to offer. For us, this translates to kids staying up past bedtime catching fireflies, eating breakfast on our porch, and enjoying evenings with roaring bonfires. I love this time of year. It is the season to "whistle while we work." After taking a deep breath from the busyness of spring, we get to sit back and watch the crops grow to full maturity. It comes with a deep feeling of gratitude that we long to share with others through hospitality.

One night we gathered to show our appreciation—for great pie! We had a favorite pie party, and our entire family was the reason for the celebration. Our pie night first started as a spontaneous, casual gathering for no particular reason other than to be together. How often do we have those days? With birthday parties and holidays, I can get so lost in the preparations that I lose sight of the true purpose of gathering. I get caught up in those small details that really don't matter. I don't have to have the perfect cake or party decorations. Why is it so important to me to have things polished that most other people won't even see?

My own pride and judgment can surface if my focus is more on entertaining and less on opening my home in true hospitality. I will ask myself, *Isn't this supposed to be a fun-loving celebration?* But God is not asking me to start a cleaning business, and gatherings are not about the opportunity to entertain. I am to wholeheartedly welcome others into godly relationships.

When I see that it is not about the setting but the environment of warmth and judgment-free zones, the picture becomes clear: if I desire for Christ's love to be apparent to all who come to my gatherings, the small details, preparations, insecurities, and anxieties surrounding it will fade away. How? Because as I settle into what entertaining means (for the benefit of others) I can easily see how hospitality benefits *me*. It's for me to open up my heart, share what I can with someone else, and have my life impacted by the presence of others.

Our pie night was a great example of this simple hospitality. My mother-in-law, Denise, opened her home in a warm, inviting way. Her heart was ready to humbly serve the Lord by intentionally sharing love with us and welcoming us into her home not for her sake but for ours. She kept it easy with the simple theme of "our favorite pies." By asking everyone to share about their pie and the memories that came with it, Denise showed she cared about all of our stories.

Shelby

I've never met a pie I didn't like. Some may consider it a problem; I consider it a blessing. I enjoy pie so much that I even request it for my birthday instead of cake. So, when the idea of having a favorite pie night was suggested, I immediately jumped on board.

Our laid-back gathering took place in the comforts of a cozy farm backyard in Iowa. Denise's yard and landscaping are comfortable and welcoming, featuring a wooden table in the center for all to gather together. The pies were placed right on that table in the middle of the yard, easy to spot when you walked out the back door, with a few of them up on pretty pedestal cake stands to give a festive feel.

We each brought a favorite pie or two to share; there were seven delicious pies that evening, and no two were the same. When I think back on that evening, I don't remember if Denise's yard was mowed. I don't recall if the pie was served on nice china or paper plates. I don't remember which pie looked the best or even tasted the best. What I do remember was that I looked forward to gathering at the end of the day with some of my favorite people and some delicious pies. It wasn't about the presentation but the *presence*.

Ordinary is best sustained when there's celebration in the middle of it.

The kids played outside, enjoying the fresh air, four-wheelers, and tree swing. The adults relaxed with a glass of cool lemonade and conversation. We then jumped into the pies (not literally) by starting off with a very informal taste contest. Everyone was allowed a sliver of any of the pies they thought they'd like, and then we voted for our favorite. On this evening, I realized my young son, Thomas, had inherited my love for pie. He tried every single pie and then went back for more. Thomas had a hard time choosing his favorite, but Grandma De's cherry pie and the "key line" were among his top contenders.

After our contest ended, we dug in for a real-sized slice or two of our favorites and conversed about the different pies and the memories they evoked. Many of the pie recipes had been handed down for generations. Annie talked about her homespun, humble, unassuming Grandma Maxine and the countless pies she made from the apples picked in her own orchard. Her rustic pies were indicative of her personality—not fancy and never perfect. But they were wonderfully delicious with an unbeatable crust. On the other hand, Grandma Betty had perfected her mile-high meringue on her lemon pies. She valued quality and achievement in all things in life, and even her pies demonstrated that. While these pies were so different, they were equally special and delicious. Diversity in tastes and offerings can lead to unity around the table.

My husband and his brother talked about climbing high on shaky ladders into the sour cherry tree in our backyard. We laughed about how the danger was worth the delicious reward of De's cherry pie. We talked about Aunt Kay's amazing Simple Pie Crust, which led to a story about Denise actually shoving a piece of pie into her brother's face at a birthday party years ago. Molly shared that she loved key lime pie because it reminded her of birthdays spent on the balmy sandy beaches in Florida as a kid. Denise shared about how her mother required her to know how to make a pie before becoming engaged to my father-in-law, and that she has been making Coconut Cream Pie for him for over forty years now.

Reflecting on the conversation and the fun of having a pie "potluck" at the end of a long, ordinary day reminded me of how essential it is to not let things slip into "just getting by" but to stop and celebrate before moving on to the next thing. Sometimes life can get so rigorous that I think we forget to enjoy it, and we forget to join with others. We think about them, but are we willing to invite them into our less-than-perfect homes? We neglect to be hospitable because it seems easier not to be. And yet I've often noticed that after we have or host a gathering, I think, *I'm so glad we did that.*

Through the simple hospitality shown by Denise, we gained a joyful confirmation of why we gather together. No fancy menu or fancy location was needed; we simply gathered together and delighted in each other's company. Showing love can take place in even the most ordinary days when we choose to resemble Jesus, who gives us the provisions to share with others. When we open our door, no matter what it looks like inside, we are saying to others, "I celebrate you, not the accomplishment of what my house looks like," and we are allowing God to not only transform our ordinary days but also our hearts and homes. Hospitality isn't a state of readiness; it's a practice of humility.

A Place at His Table

Molly

The idea of hospitality brings up different images for each of us, doesn't it? For some it brings panic. For others it's a deeply rooted desire to love but not feeling capable due to time constraints. I typically think of an elaborate party that involves an excessive amount of planning and preparing. Like Shelby discussed, that often keeps me from being more hospitable. But when Paul instructs us to "practice hospitality" in Romans 12:13, I'm reminded of my need to let go of the image that says, *This is going to take up a lot of time and be difficult.*

The more I learn, and the more I read what the Bible teaches us about loving others, I realize hospitality is actually quite simple. Jesus said, "My command is this: Love each other as I have loved you" (John 15:12). It begins with us— our love and our willingness to set aside our agenda for another. The heart of a giver is all that's required.

Jesus is our greatest example of hospitality, and when we imitate him, we are walking out what he has taught us. We see examples in Matthew where he brings life to the dead, shows compassion to the lost, and brings comfort to the weary. We also find him frying fish on the beach with his disciples, feeding bread to the hungry on the hillside, and eating with tax collectors. Even just before his death, he broke bread with his closest friends and told them to keep doing this to remember him. Jesus's sacrifice of his life signaled his love. Showing love and joining in the life of others is what Jesus did so well. He is the definition of hospitality.

Hospitality is loving, caring, and welcoming. Hospitality is listening, inviting, and serving. Hospitality is being generous. When I simply open my house to others, I am opening my soul to receive and minister to others.

When I reflect back on our favorite pie party, I think about how Denise was loving through serving. Her focus was less on the event and more on the people. There was no agenda, other than valuing one another (and tasting pies!).

Denise displayed care by asking meaningful questions and opening up a time for sharing, listening, and even praying together.

I realized that this day was just an ordinary evening *until* it became a meaningful one. And what transformed this day from ordinary to meaningful was the hospitality of Christ! When Christ is at the center of the table, when he is invited into a gathering and we are loving one another, meaningful moments occur. When we turn our hearts toward *How do I help others feel seen?* rather than *How do I get through another meal?* we have entered the way of celebration.

Key Ingredients

Annie

After experiencing hospitality from my mom during the favorite pie party and thinking about what the Bible has to say about opening up our hearts to show love, I got to thinking about some practical ways we can bring hospitality into our already full lives. I'm often one to measure things in volume—food, budget, laundry—so I tend to think I have to do something *huge* to be hospitable. But I've learned it doesn't have to be big. Guests are actually relieved when it's quite simple, because it means they don't have to do something big either. See how good this is for all of us? I take the pressure off you—you take the pressure off me!

There are many ideas you can easily incorporate into your life to offer this type of hospitality.

Keep It Simple

I was recently invited to a book club by a new friend. The hostess texted me the day of the gathering to say, "I'm so glad you're coming! Just wear your comfiest clothes." That text relieved my anxieties about going to a new group. My friend let me know that it was important I was coming and that she was more concerned about the true me than a perfect outfit. When I arrived, I was greeted with a warm hug and a "Welcome! I'm so glad you're here!" She proceeded to offer me a cup of coffee and a treat from a plate full of . . . Oreos!

Those Oreos and the fact that the other ladies were wearing favorite yoga pants and hanging out together on the couch made the evening comfortable and low-key. The relaxed atmosphere took the attention off of food, clothes, or home decor and instead helped us focus on each other and some great conversation. This "come as you are and be yourself" attitude exhibited the love of Christ to me.

In what ways can you show hospitality in a similar, comfortable way?

» Meet at a park and bring a picnic to share. When my kids were little, I invited friends to meet at a community center that had a play structure. We'd visit over a cup of coffee while keeping an eye on the kids. No one will feel any less "loved" because you aren't meeting at your home.

» Be spontaneous and casually invite people over. Last-minute often works better for some folks than weeks of planning. Intentionally focus more on the people rather than on the food and preparations.

» Host a "leisure club," "informal book group," or other gathering around a purpose and serve foods you can pick up at the grocery store. When your friends see that you didn't stress, they'll feel more at ease and open to conversation.

» Like my friend did, text your guests before they arrive to say, "I'm glad you're coming. Just wear your comfiest clothes!" Your text might also say, "Don't worry about childcare—come with your kids!" or "Come when you can!" Use texts as an encouraging way to show others you value them and their presence at your gathering.

» Have some light, casual music playing in the background. Music sets the tone for the environment and helps guests (and hosts) feel more at ease.

Think Ahead—Curate Conversation

We live in a culture where conversations can easily stay at a surface level. We ask, "How are you?" and expect to always hear, "Fine." But don't you think we are meant to show Christ's love by being more intentional with our conversation? Being purposeful in listening, making eye contact, and asking deeper questions are effective ways to show hospitality.

>> Ask purposeful questions. As Colossians 4:6 tells us, let's keep our conversations "seasoned with salt." Instead of "How are you?" try: "What are you enjoying about summer?" "What are you loving right now?" "What is something you have discovered recently?"

>> If your gathering is a comfortable place to do so, try some faith-based questions. Among fellow believers, consider asking, "What are you learning about God lately?" Ask God to help you to be sensitive about knowing when to talk about your faith and when not to. He promises to give us the words to say. If you're not sure where another may be in their walk with the Lord, simply be willing to listen and let the person speak in whatever way makes them comfortable.

>> Keep a box of question cards on your coffee table. These can be purchased or printed from websites. We've had lots of great conversations with friends over the years that began by pulling out a card that asked something quirky, such as, "What is the strangest thing you've ever eaten?"

>> Remember to extend hospitality to young guests by having some toys ready for them to play with. Even though my girls have outgrown playing with dolls, I keep a tote of their favorite dolls and clothes easily accessible so other little girls immediately feel comfortable in our home. Be creative in what you can offer to the children, which may just allow their parents to relax and join in more conversation with other adults.

>> Purposefully place younger and older guests together for deeper discussions by making place cards for your table. This is an easy ignitor for discipling, mentoring, and learning to take place.

Host a "Favorite" Party

A favorite pie party just seemed fitting for us, but really it could be anything you enjoy. Everyone contributes by adding their personality and flair to the event, even if you don't bake or if it's not about a favorite dish. It could be a favorite craft or favorite way to join forces by creating something for a local ministry you're sponsoring. We all need more reasons to celebrate, and doing it together is the best.

» Consider any of these "favorite" events: pies, cookies (decorate them together!), pizza, ice cream sundaes, games.

» If children will be present, get them involved in setting the table, filling water glasses, taking coats, starting off the conversation, and assisting with plates and dishes. Kids feel good when they can contribute.

>> Plan an activity such as painting rocks, having a beanbag toss, or another hands-on activity for all ages. Some ideas include baking, cake decorating, sewing, painting, sign painting, gardening, or canning.

>> Use something other than everyday dishes to serve: this could be seasonal paper plates, colorful Fiestaware, vintage pieces, or just setting out a few cake pedestals for serving and display.

Show Love in Small Ways

Hospitality does not always have to involve hosting; often it's just observing, paying attention, and taking a small action. If I know I won't have time to meet with someone, I'll often set a reminder to follow up with them later. We can also pray for others and even text them a prayer or a Scripture to let them know we are thinking of them. You might want to write down birthdays and special events and send notes of encouragement prior to when it might show up on Facebook. (*Wink.*)

It is easy to *say* that because of our faith and love of God we desire to show his love and hospitality to others, but we must put feet to our faith and *act* in God's love, as the apostle James says: "Show me your faith without deeds, and I will show you my faith by my deeds" (James 2:18).

Hopefully these ideas will inspire you to do just that.

>> Keep a notebook with information about your family and friends to remember something specific your guests enjoy, such as tea or a favorite food. Include important birthdays, events, and prayer requests.

>> Be willing to notice someone's demeanor and ask a tough question. "You seem a little tired today. Is everything okay?" "Is there anything I could pray about for you?" I know that this can be uncomfortable, but opening up a safe place for someone to share can be life-changing. Jesus says in John 13:35, "By this everyone will know that you are my disciples, if you love one another."

» Send friends home with something homemade or thoughtful. When our neighbor has us over for dinner, she always sends us home with the leftovers. It's unbelievably generous! A thank-you card is always a simple yet effective gesture. Make cards ahead of time to send with your guests on their way home, or if you're the guest, bring one as a thank-you gesture to your host. Such small but well-thought-out gestures can make such a difference in life.

» Budget hack—ask God to show you what you could give; he will help! Here are a few ideas: a seasonal printable (Pinterest!), a beautifully handwritten verse (YouTube videos can teach you how), flowers cut from your yard, some bread dough with directions on how to bake a delicious loaf of bread, a watercolor that you've painted, or a homemade coupon to babysit a friend's children for a few hours.

» Fresh flowers are a beautiful blessing. Have these in your home as a welcome invitation for guests, and be ready to give them away after the gathering is over. "I'm so glad you came tonight. I would love to send some flowers home with you!" Or, if you're the guest, bring flowers as a gesture of gratitude for being invited.

» Give a seasonal gift that really shows you care. Whenever I visit IKEA, I stock up on the seasonal napkins and dish towels from the huge marketplace bins. These make a fun, bright, effortless gift that can be sent home at the end of an event, and might even spur others on to host something in their home.

» Prepare some cookie dough, shape it into balls, and freeze. You'll be ready to make warm, delicious cookies if someone unexpectedly "drops in," and you'll also be prepared to spontaneously invite a friend into your home.

Apron Application

Denise

1. Can you think of a time when you focused on entertaining instead of hospitality? There have been times when I intentionally declined an opportunity to invite someone in because my house was not in perfect order. Now I keep Windex and paper towels in my bathroom for a one-minute wipe down.

2. Who could you share God's love with today? This week? Who has God placed on your heart to show his love and care? Pray specifically for this relationship. Then find a simple way to show hospitality to them.

3. If asked, would friends say you were an intentional listener? Tender care draws people in quickly. I have created a section in a binder titled "Relationships." As I learn new details about a friend, loved one, or new acquaintance, I quickly jot them down. It's good to hear, "You remembered!"

4. What ways can you show gratitude to the Lord today? Remember to thank him. If he is calling you to show hospitality, write down what you are feeling as you pray.

Prayer

Dear Jesus, you have asked me to show love and draw those around me to you. Please help me be filled with your love by welcoming others into my heart and being ready to offer something inviting and refreshing to them, whether it be food, an activity, or just simply talking. Help me know when to speak and when to listen. And help me see and use my gifts of home, food, and friendly conversation to bring refreshment to someone else's soul. Help me not worry about the imperfections and distractions but instead intentionally point people to your perfect love. Grant me a deeper desire to reach out and connect with those you have placed in my sphere of influence. Help me be a refreshment to them. I know they are thirsty for your love, just like me.

Gather at Your Table

Pies and summer just go together here in rural Iowa, but if that's not your thing, you could have another type of "favorite" party. Keep it simple, and maybe even be spontaneous with your event. Be creative with the setting. Think of a little token you can send home with guests.

Simple Pie Crust

Prep: 10 minutes
+ 30 minutes chill time
Bake: 8-10 minutes
Yield: 1 pie crust

1 cup	all-purpose flour
¼ tsp	salt
½ cup	cold butter or margarine, cubed (1 stick)
¼ cup	milk

Directions

1. Combine flour and salt in a mixing bowl. With a pastry blender or two table knives held together, cut in the cubes of butter until well blended, about pea-sized coarse crumbs.
2. Add in milk slowly and stir to make dough.
3. Cover with plastic wrap and refrigerate for 30 minutes before rolling. On generously floured surface, roll out dough into a circle about an inch larger than your pie plate, then press into plate with floured hands. Dough can also be well-wrapped and refrigerated for several days, or frozen for up to three months.

   Note: To make a prebaked crust, pierce the bottom and sides of crust with a fork before baking. Bake at 425° for 8–10 minutes, until golden brown.

   This dough is softer than a regular pie crust and is easier to handle.

Coconut Cream Pie

Prep time: 15 minutes
+ 2 hours chill time
Cook time: 15 minutes
Yield: 8–10 servings

1	Simple Pie Crust, prebaked and cooled
¾ cup	sugar
⅓ cup	all-purpose flour
¼ tsp	salt
2 cups	milk (I use 1%)
3	egg yolks, slightly beaten
2 Tbs	butter
1 tsp	vanilla extract
1½ cups	moist sweetened flaked coconut
2 cups	homemade whipped cream or whipped topping

Directions

1. In saucepan, stir together sugar, flour, and salt. Over medium heat, slowly stir in milk.
2. Bring to a boil. Stir constantly while boiling gently for 2 minutes.
3. Remove from heat and combine 2 Tbs hot mixture with egg yolks. Stir to combine, then pour the tempered egg yolk mixture back into the saucepan. Stirring constantly, bring back to a boil, and cook for 2 more minutes.
4. Remove from heat. Stir in butter and vanilla, then coconut, until fully melted and combined; let cool. Pour filling into crust.
5. Cover with plastic wrap and refrigerate at least 2 hours before serving. Add homemade whipped cream or whipped topping.

   Variation: use purchased mini phyllo dough cups in lieu of pie crust for bite-sized pies.

Banana Cream Pie

Prep time: 15 minutes
+ 2–3 hours chill time
Cook time: 15 minutes
Yield: 8–10 servings

1	Simple Pie Crust or frozen pie crust, prebaked and cooled
4–5	bananas, sliced (optional: reserve ½ banana for garnish)
¾ cup	sugar
⅓ cup	all-purpose flour
¼ tsp	salt
2 cups	milk
3	egg yolks, slightly beaten
2 Tbs	butter
1 tsp	vanilla
2 cups	homemade whipped cream or whipped topping

other optional garnishes: slivered almonds, bananas, chocolate syrup

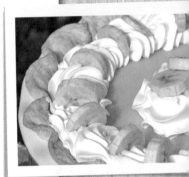

Directions

1. Slice bananas and place in crust. Layer in a circular form, starting on the outer edge and working to the middle.
2. In a heavy bottomed saucepan, combine sugar, flour, and salt. Gradually stir in milk. Cook and stir over medium heat until bubbly, then stir for 2 additional minutes. Remove from heat.
3. Stir 2 Tbs of hot mixture into egg yolks; immediately return tempered yolk mixture to hot mixture. Bring back to a boil and cook about 2 more minutes or until thickened, stirring constantly so it doesn't burn. Remove from heat. Add butter and vanilla and stir until fully melted and combined.
4. Pour filling on top of bananas in pie crust.
5. Refrigerate for 2–3 hours, until thick and firm. Top with whipped cream or whipped topping. Keep refrigerated until ready to eat.

Jenny shares: Summertime is a time of going outside and taking advantage of the nice warm sunshine that God provides us. I love the long days. Everyone enjoys a summer party when there are pies involved! My favorite pie was the French Chocolate. There were so many delicious ones to choose from.

French Chocolate Pie

Prep time: 15 minutes
+ 2 hours chill time
Cook time: 12 minutes
Yield: 8–10 servings

1	Simple Pie Crust, prebaked and cooled
½ cup	butter, softened (1 stick)
¾ cup	sugar
2 oz.	unsweetened baking chocolate, melted and cooled
2	eggs
4 cups	whipped topping, divided

Directions

1. Cream butter with sugar. Stir in the cooled melted chocolate.
2. One at a time, add eggs. Beat at high speed for 5 minutes after each addition.
3. Fold in 2 cups whipped topping. Pour into prebaked pie crust. Chill until firm, about 2 hours.
4. Top with remaining whipped topping and garnish with chocolate shavings, if desired.

   Note: This pie can be frozen for 1–2 days. Let thaw for about an hour before serving.

Grandma Betty's (Easiest Ever) Key Lime Pie

Prep time: 5 minutes
+ 1 hour chill time
Yield: 8–10 servings

1	graham cracker crust, store-bought or homemade
1 (14 oz.) can	sweetened condensed milk
16 oz.	whipped topping
⅓ cup	key lime juice (fresh or bottled)
	lime slices to garnish, optional

Directions

1. To make a graham cracker crust, in a small bowl toss together 2 cups graham crumbs, ½ cup melted butter, and 2 Tbs sugar. Press mixture into bottom and 2 inches up sides of a 9-inch pie pan. Chill in freezer while preparing the filling.
2. Stir together condensed milk, whipped topping, and lime juice.
3. Spread mixture in pie crust and refrigerate until cool, at least 1 hour.
4. Top with more whipped topping and garnish with lime slices, if desired.

Cherry Pie

Prep time: 25 minutes
Cook time: 40–50 minutes
Yield: 8-10 servings

2	Simple Pie Crusts, unbaked
4–5 cups	sour cherries, drained well (can use frozen if out of season; thaw)
1–2 tsp	almond extract
¼ tsp	salt
¼ cup	all-purpose flour
1½ cups	sugar
1 Tbs	butter, cubed

Directions

1. Preheat oven to 425°.
2. Mix together cherries, almond extract, salt, flour, and sugar.
3. Place one crust in pie pan and pour filling into crust. Dot with butter.
4. Cut remaining crust into lattice strips. Try to make them all the same width. I generally have 6 strips going one direction, or 12 strips total (though it can be more or less). Strips should be long enough to hang over the edge a little. Place 6 strips across the pie, in one direction; do this lightly, as you will move some of them To place strips in the opposite direction, lay back every other strip you just placed and weave a strip in, laying it in the middle and working toward one side; then moving from the middle to the other side. Trim overhanging strips and incorporate by finishing the edges and crimp crusts together. With your hand, wet top of crust with a little water and sprinkle with sugar.
5. Bake for 40–50 minutes, until filling is bubbling around the edges. Cover the edges with foil until last 10 minutes to keep crust from burning.

Fresh Peach Blueberry Pie

Prep time: 25 minutes
Cook time: 40–50 minutes
Yield: 8–10 servings

2	Simple Pie Crusts, unbaked
6 cups	fresh peaches (approx. 8–10), blanched, peeled, and sliced
1 tsp	lemon juice
¾ cup	fresh blueberries (frozen works in a pinch)
⅓ cup	all-purpose flour
3 tsp	almond extract
pinch	ground cinnamon
1¼ cup	sugar, divided
1 Tbs	butter, cubed

Directions

1. Preheat oven to 425°.
2. In a large bowl, stir together peaches and lemon juice; add blueberries.
3. Mix in flour, almond extract, cinnamon, and all but 1 Tbs of the sugar. Turn into a pastry-lined pie plate and dot with butter.
4. Add top crust and make slits in it, or a design of your choice. Flute the edges with your favorite design, making sure to seal the top and bottom crusts together.
5. With your hand, wet the top crust with a few drips of water and sprinkle with reserved Tbs sugar (or sprinkle with a little almond extract).
6. Cover crust loosely with a sheet of aluminum foil and bake for 30 minutes. Remove foil and bake for another 10–20 minutes. Serve warm and with vanilla ice cream, if desired.

Strawberry Cream Cheese Slab Pie

1 box	refrigerated pie crust (2 crusts) or 2 Simple Pie Crusts
16 oz.	cream cheese, softened
⅔ cup	sugar
1 Tbs	milk
6 cups	fresh strawberries, sliced
1 cup	strawberry glaze (in the produce section next to strawberries)

Prep time: 20 minutes
+ 2 hours chill time
Cook time: 10–12 minutes
Yield: 16 servings

Directions

1. Preheat oven to 450°.
2. Place pie crust dough on a lightly floured surface. (If using packaged crust, unroll them and stack on top of each other.) With a rolling pin, roll into a 17x12 rectangle to fit into a 15x10 baking sheet. Make sure to roll dough evenly so it will bake evenly. Press into ungreased pan, all the way into the corners. Crimp edges and prick entire crust with a fork.
3. Bake 10–12 minutes or until golden brown. Cool completely.
4. Beat cream cheese, sugar, and milk until smooth. Spread evenly on cooled crust. Refrigerate until set, about 1 hour.
5. Gently mix sliced strawberries and strawberry glaze and spread evenly over cream cheese.
6. Cover and refrigerate. Chill for at least 1 hour before serving.

Anniversary Picnic & Bike Ride

*Commemorating the
Faithfulness of God*

De's Baked Beans

Easy Pasta Salad

Italian Wedding Cake

Southern Fried Chicken

Grandma Betty's Refrigerator Rolls

Fresh Freezer Corn—straight from the corn factory!

Homemade Sweet Tea

Shelby

The Lord has been faithful to all of us in so many ways. He blesses us, protects us, teaches us, and grows us. His love for us is never failing. We all face various trials and struggles throughout our lives, and during these times it's especially important to remember how faithful God has been.

> *I will give thanks to you, LORD, with all my heart;*
> *I will tell of all your wonderful deeds. (Ps. 9:1)*

Some milestones in our lives are greater than others, and we want to commemorate these significant events in a special way. We want to celebrate them and create a memory so we won't forget. In the midst of our year of gatherings, my father-in-law, Stan, and mother-in-law, Denise, reached a marriage milestone—their forty-fifth wedding anniversary. We knew we wanted to plan something extra special for them, to celebrate.

We're all so thankful for the great example of Christian marriage they've set and also for the way they both live out their faith every day. We developed a plan to surprise them with a gathering. We talked about various ideas and agreed upon a family picnic and bike ride; the two things they enjoy most are their family and the outdoors. We quickly got to work on planning a menu and deciding who was bringing each item. Jenny snuck into their shed and cleaned up their bikes, then secretly loaded them into the back of Bill's truck.

The anticipated day arrived, and we were all eager for the celebration to begin. As far as Stan and Denise went, all they knew was when to arrive and what to wear.

Denise

A few days before our forty-fifth wedding anniversary, the kids informed Mr. Farmer and me that they were doing a little something for us. "Be at Bill and Shelby's by 4:00 p.m., dressed in casual clothing," we were told. We looked at each other, smiled, and said, "Okay!"

We arrived at their house promptly at four. As we walked into the garage, I saw bike wheels sticking up out of the box of their pickup. *I love biking!* I love the wind on my face with my hair flying behind. I don't enjoy the hills, but they certainly won't stop me from getting on a bike.

Bill and Shelby told us they would lead the way to where the family was converging, at a state park about thirty miles away. When we pulled up, we saw all seventeen of us were there, with bikes and kiddy trailers—every attachment you can think of so that even the littlest ones could caravan with us. Our kids were thrilled to have kept this big event a secret. Our grandkids were whoopin' and hollerin' all over the place.

Before the bike ride, we needed to fuel up. The kids had planned a perfect picnic for us. They each pitched in, and we had some scrumptious fried chicken and homemade sides. The girls swiftly set a beautiful picnic table and presented us with a delicious tiered cake, which was used as the centerpiece. In a flash we were all engaged in eating delicious food and enjoying the fresh air and warm and rambunctious conversation as we sat atop a hillside overlooking the lake. I pinched myself and dabbed a tear with my sleeve. It truly was a grand celebration, one we'll never forget.

When the last piece of finger-licking-good chicken was gone, we climbed the hill to our bikes and, in a flash, all nineteen of us were in a very long line, beginning our tour of the lake on a trail that wrapped all the way around it, about four miles. What a joy it was to look behind me and see so many smiling faces. When we returned, the children played on the playground equipment while the table was graced with the bouquet of flowers and a beautiful anniversary cake. Together, Stan and I cut the cake. We were then presented with a large gift to unwrap. We tore open the paper and found a lovely framed portrait of our family that had been taken a couple weeks before in our orchard—our backyard. It was a perfect gift at a perfect anniversary party in a perfect setting with all our family—yes, a perfect scene of God's beautiful handiwork. The memories of that special party will last forever. And it was God's idea. Sure, he left the kids to do the planning and follow-through of this event, but he's the one who started the observance of commitments, vows, dedications, and remembrances of grand happenings. He asks us to pause and remember—in this case the marriage vows and commitment made forty years previous. *Thank you, Father, that we can stop and celebrate and relive the commitment we made so long ago. And thank you, Father, for letting us enjoy forty years of marriage together, enjoying a multitude of family blessings.*

> *For you make me glad by your deeds, Lord;*
> *I sing for joy at what your hands have done. (Ps. 92:4)*

A Place at His Table

Annie

I don't know about you, but sometimes it's easier for me to place my focus on the difficulties and disappointments in life than to remember God's blessings, answers to prayer, and daily provision.

Repeatedly in Scripture, God tells us to "remember the deeds of the Lord" (Ps. 77:11), to "not forget the things your eyes have seen" (Deut. 4:9), and to give thanks. I love the story from Joshua 4, which details what happens after God has done a miracle for his children: he actually stopped the flow of the Jordan River so the nation of Israel could cross. Joshua then tells twelve men to place memorial stones to help the people forever remember God's mighty deed (vv. 1–9). I especially love verse 6: "When your children ask you, 'What do these stones mean?'" It shows that the stones will prompt God's people to tell their children about his faithfulness.

Why do you think it was so important for the Israelites to remember God's faithfulness? And why is it so important for us to remember what God has done? Quite simply, remembering increases faith. When things are hard and doubts come, remembering helps us trust that God is there and that he will come through again. I love how Charles Spurgeon explains this truth. He said, "Memory is a fit handmaid for faith. When faith has its seven years of famine, memory like Joseph in Egypt opens her granaries."[1]

> *Remember the former things, those of long ago;*
> *I am God, and there is no other;*
> *I am God, and there is none like me. (Isa. 46:9)*

How can we be prompted to remember and retell about God's faithfulness to our children and grandchildren? For our family, planning a special gathering that will be enjoyed, photographed, and reminisced over forever is a concrete way to remember the deeds of the Lord. This is why my parents' anniversary picnic and bike ride event was so significant. When we look at pictures and share memories from that day, we get to say to our kids, "God has been so faithful to our family. Your grandparents have had so many wonderful years together."

And the most important thing to recount to my kids and grandkids? The work that Jesus did on the cross for me. Together with our children, we can sing, "Jesus sought me when a stranger, wandering from the fold of God; he, to rescue me from danger, interposed his precious blood."[2]

Key Ingredients

Molly

Why do we honor milestones? Because they are an affirmation of our accomplishments and growth. Celebrations don't always have to include cake, candles, a lot of people, and gifts. They can be modestly taking the time to appreciate, pause, and reflect. However big or small the milestone, it's essential to reflect on the importance of the relationship and create a time for thanksgiving and often also a time for deep gratitude.

Capitalize on Milestones

Wedding anniversaries. These are often celebrated by the married couple via a date, a trip, and/or a time of reflection on the wedding date. Some may go to the extent of renewing their vows, while others may create a party and invite family and friends to be a part of it.

Anniversary book—I was given an anniversary book as a gift for our wedding. It is a wonderful tool for us because with each anniversary it provides space to write in the year, the tradition that goes along with it, and what we did.

Card shower—If a full-blown party isn't really your thing, having a card shower can be an effective way to celebrate a special couple. In addition to our anniversary picnic, we also sent out an email to all friends and family inviting them to join in sending cards to the honored couple.

Birthdays. I can't think of one birthday not celebrated in my life. Some were more grandiose than others, but each and every one of them was celebrated. The older I get, the more I don't feel the need for a birthday party. However, through cards, gifts, and the physical presence of others, I enjoy coming together. There is thankfulness for what lies ahead and remembrance of memories past.

Birthday letter—Another way to remember someone and their upcoming birthday is to write them a letter to be saved. This can include a record of traits you enjoy about them and any specific memories or reflections from the past year.

Birthday interview—This a cute and fun way to learn about your child (or friend or family member). Have a yearly interview with some basic questions for them to fill out. Reflect back over the years and see how things change.

Graduations. Whether a high school, college, or other program graduation, it deserves celebration.

Scrapbook—My mom was great about collecting all of the pieces about me from school over the years. She had every class photo, blue ribbon, newspaper clipping—not to mention cards that were given to me and even my old Christmas lists. I have the same intentions for my kids, and now I realize how important these are because they show us our capabilities and how we have developed.[3]

Make It a Surprise

Surprises come in many forms and can almost be more exhilarating for those doing the planning. The element of surprise keeps us reeling and adds a little extra wonder to the event, whether it's a large party with family, friends, and coworkers or a small surprise like, "I'm taking you out for dinner tonight."

Preserve the Memories

Sometimes I can forget the importance of holding on to things and saving items. I can tell myself, *I have stored up the memory in my mind. Why go through the extra effort of keeping photos or cards?* Memories can sometimes fade. I am so touched when I look back through a photo album or I find a gift and remember who it was from and why. It makes the celebration even more significant when we have those tangible items to help us retain the memories, feelings, people, and sometimes even smells.

Through song. Music is something that catches me off guard. It astonishes me how it sets my mood and lightens my heart. When I hear music or song associated with a certain memory, often it all comes back to me—I can picture the setting and who I was with, what we were doing, and the feeling I had at the time.

Through journaling and cards. During my elementary years, I journaled frequently. I would write pages about traveling or just make up my own stories. I even wrote letters to myself, purposefully hid them in a drawer, and then surprised myself with them a year later. Now as a busy adult, I can lose sight of this. But I am enamored when I reread saved cards from grandparents (who have now passed) or even notes from friends or parents. There is something special about seeing their handwriting that makes me feel they are with me again in that moment.

Through photos. Photos capture exact moments in time. I can often recall the thoughts and feelings I had at the exact moment a photo was taken, even years later. Photos and photo albums are an assurance of our memories and are a beautiful reminder of the Lord's faithfulness.

Through symbolic representation. This can be done in many forms and may include "placing an Ebenezer stone" for milestones, pouring sand at weddings to show unity, using stones to represent a family or group, or planting bushes or trees as a memorial or remembrance.

Apron Application

 Shelby ——————

1. What significant milestones do you or your loved ones have coming up? What are some ways you can commemorate these bigger moments?

2. Read Psalm 77:11: "I will remember the deeds of the LORD; yes, I will remember your miracles of long ago." Spend a few minutes in silence reflecting on the good deeds God has done for you.

3. In hindsight, what difficult life situations has God seen you through? What blessings has God given you? How has God shown you his faithfulness during both scenarios?

4. What are some ways you can teach younger generations about the faithfulness of God?

5. We are called to "give thanks in all circumstances; for this is God's will for [us] in Christ Jesus" (1 Thess. 5:18). Is there a circumstance you haven't given thanks for? Lay that down today and thank the Lord.

Prayer

Dear Lord, we thank you for your continued faithfulness. We ask that you grant us continued wisdom to pull from significant life experiences and the needed humility to lean on you in times of need. Help us show gratitude in all seasons. May our faith continue to grow with each day and through each experience you bless us with. Let us always remember to commemorate the big milestones in our lives and give thanks to you for the work you have done. We hope to honor you by teaching and showing future generations demonstrations of your goodness. In Jesus's name we pray, Amen.

Gather at Your Table

Oh, how I (Denise) love surprises. This outdoor party is one we will never forget. Yes, it took a little planning, but boy did Mr. Farmer and I feel so special and so loved. Whether it's a birthday, an anniversary, or another day to commemorate, just do it! Making others feel special brings joy to one and all. You can keep it simple by adding some store-bought items.

De's Baked Beans

Prep time: 5 minutes
Cook time: 45–60 minutes
Yield: 8–10 servings

1 (28 oz.) can   pork and beans, drained
¼ cup   onion, chopped
¼ cup   ketchup
⅓ cup   brown sugar
3–4 slices   hickory smoked bacon, chopped into 2-inch pieces

Directions

1. Preheat oven to 350°.
2. Combine beans, onion, ketchup, and brown sugar in a large mixing bowl. Stir well. Pour into 2 qt. casserole dish.
3. Top with bacon pieces. Bake for 45–60 minutes, until bubbly.

Easy Pasta Salad

Prep time: 15 minutes
Cook time: 15 minutes
Yield: 8–10 servings

1 lb.   pasta of choice
6–8 oz.   cheese, cubed (such as mild cheddar or Colby jack)
½ cup   raw veggies, chopped (such as peppers, carrots, and broccoli)

For dressing

16 oz.   creamy Italian dressing
¾ cup   sugar
2 tsp   prepared yellow mustard

Directions

1. Cook pasta according to package directions, drain, and allow to cool.
2. Add selected cheese and veggies to pasta; mix together.
3. Whisk together dressing ingredients and pour over pasta and vegetables; stir to combine.
4. Cover and refrigerate until ready to serve.

Italian Wedding Cake

Prep time: 30 minutes
Cook time: 20 minutes
Yield: 10-12 servings

For cake

1 box	white cake mix
1 cup	shredded sweetened coconut
½ cup	black walnuts, finely chopped
2 tsp	almond extract
1 tsp	butter flavoring

For decorator's frosting

½ cup	vegetable shortening
7½ cups	powdered sugar
¼–½ cup	milk
1½ tsp	clear vanilla extract
½ tsp	almond extract
½ cup	butter, softened (1 stick)

Directions

1. Preheat oven and mix cake batter according to package instructions, omitting egg yolks if called for.
2. Add coconut, walnuts, almond extract, and butter flavoring to batter.
3. Grease two 9-inch baking pans with cooking spray (or desired equivalent) and pour batter into pans.
4. Bake according to package instructions. Cool cake completely.
5. For frosting, blend together shortening, butter, powdered sugar, and ¼ cup milk. Add in vanilla and almond extracts. Add more milk if needed to reach desired consistency. Frost cake as desired.

Southern Fried Chicken

Prep time: 10 minutes
Cook time: 30–45 minutes
Yield: 6–8 servings

2 lbs.	raw chicken pieces, as desired
½ cup	vegetable oil (or a combination of vegetable oil and a little olive oil)
1 cup	buttermilk
1½ cups	all-purpose flour
1 tsp	seasoned salt
1 tsp	salt
1 tsp	pepper

Directions

1. Preheat oil in large skillet over medium-high heat (or to 375°).
2. Place buttermilk in one bowl and flour mixed with seasoned salt, salt, and pepper in another bowl.
3. Pat chicken dry and place one piece at a time in the buttermilk, then roll in flour, pressing flour mixture into the chicken piece well. With burner on medium-high, carefully place each piece in the hot oil and fry to a medium golden brown. Flip chicken and brown the other side, then continue to cook for approximately 30–45 minutes total. Watch the temperature of your oil; you may need to turn the burner down a bit. To ensure doneness, check the temperature of the chicken (165°), or slice open a piece near the bone and make sure there is no pink coloring on the meat.
4. Place hot chicken on paper towel–lined plate to drain excess grease. Transfer to platter and serve immediately.

— Grandma Betty's Refrigerator Rolls —

Prep time: 30 minutes
+ 2–4 hours rise time
Cook time: 20–30 minutes
Yield: approx. 2 dozen rolls

½ cup   sugar
½ cup   vegetable shortening
½ cup   boiling water
2 pkg.   active dry yeast (4½ tsp)
½ cup   warm water, 112–115°
1½ cups cold water
2   eggs, beaten
2 tsp   salt
7 cups   all-purpose flour, divided
2 Tbs   butter, melted

Directions

1. Combine sugar, shortening, and boiling water in a large bowl; stir to dissolve and cool.
2. In a small bowl, stir yeast into warm water and let sit 5–10 minutes or until dissolved.
3. Add cold water to sugar mixture in large bowl.
4. Add 2 beaten eggs, yeast mixture, and salt. Combine well.
5. With a hand mixer, beat in 4 cups of the flour. Stir in remaining 3 cups flour with a wooden spoon. Let dough rest for 1–2 hours. Dough can be refrigerated at this point for up to two weeks.
6. Shape into rolls, about golf-ball size, and place in a greased jelly roll pan or two 9x13 pans. Let rise for 1½–2 hours, until doubled in size.
7. Bake at 350° for 20–30 minutes.
8. Brush with soft butter while hot and invert onto rack to remove from pan, then turn back over and let cool a little before serving.

Fresh Freezer Corn

Prep time: 2 minutes
Cook time: 20 minutes
Yield: 6–8 serving

4 cups frozen sweet corn
3 Tbs butter
     salt and pepper, to taste

Directions

1. Empty corn into 2 qt. saucepan and cook over medium-low heat for 15 minutes, stirring occasionally.
2. Add butter, salt, and pepper, and simmer about 5 more minutes.

Homemade Sweet Tea

Prep time: 5 minutes
Cook time: 20 minutes
Yield: 6–8 (8 oz.) glasses

1 qt. water, boiling
1 family-sized tea bag
½ cup sugar or sweetener, or to taste
     lemon slices, optional

Directions

1. In a heat-safe 2 qt. pitcher, combine boiling water and sugar. Stir to dissolve.
2. Add tea bag and let steep for 20 minutes.
3. Remove tea bag.
4. Fill the pitcher with additional cold water and refrigerate.
5. Serve with lemon slices, if desired.

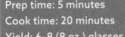

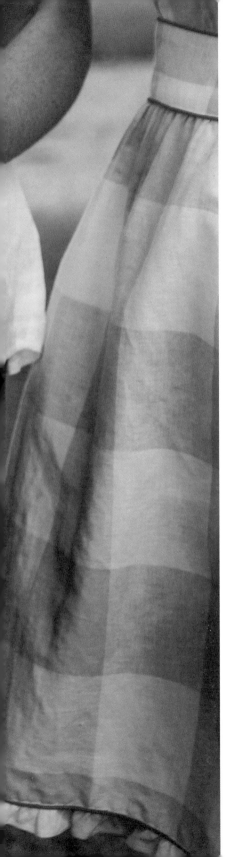

Sweet Corn Factory

*Joyfully Working Together
to Accomplish a Goal*

Shirley Temples

Homemade Ice Cream

Grandma Maxine's Peach Cobbler

Vegetable Pizza

Cold Tomato Salad

Slow Cooker Italian Beef Sandwiches

Fresh Sweet Corn with Seasoned Butters

Molly

It is late summer once again—one of my favorite times of the year. Just when I think I may be getting a little tired of one season, the next one comes knocking on the door. I like the change, but it's also hard to say goodbye to summer. I love grilling, the swimming pool, the cascading lilacs and bridal wreath, the vivid sunsets, the long sunny days, the fireflies, the bike riding, and the fresh garden produce.

But there's nothing better than this late summer period, with its abundance of fresh sweet corn and vine-ripened tomatoes. I can't tell you how often throughout the year I crave a BLT (made with those garden-ripe tomatoes, of course), fresh peaches, and creamed sweet corn—so I'm going to make sure I savor them right now.

What would I do without our annual family corn factory day? With all of us together, the workload is made light. We start by shucking corn under the shade tree. I think I may have counted a meager two ears that my young daughter shucked from the heaping pile—and then away she went, off running in the pasture. This girl always keeps me going!

Inside, more little ones are enjoying their hot beef sandwiches (the roast for which has been cooking all morning) with even more delights . . . like good old packaged cheese puffs (not to mention Shelby's peach cobbler). Once the corn is shucked, two cauldrons of water are set to boil on the stove, and it's time for our assembly process to really begin. I put twelve ears of corn in one pot and ten in the other, set the timer for eight minutes—and the lids are on! After some repetition, I think I'm getting this down; the only problem is the children are finished with their lunch and getting frisky for some playtime. The kitchen seems to be getting smaller and the potato sack bags filled with shucked corn surround my feet.

Fortunately, the playful children soon gather outdoors for a much-anticipated four-wheeler ride with its wagon hitched to the back, driven by Grandpa Stan. I hop on to help chaperone, but admittedly it's also quite an afternoon delight for me too, and I start to feel sleepy . . . the warm sunshine on my face and leaves blowing in the breeze is all it takes for me to just about shut my eyes.

When I return indoors, Denise is tending the boiling pots, Jenny is cutting corn from the cobs with the electric knife as Annie does the same with a manual knife, and Shelby is bagging the kernels—and much to my surprise, there are only ten ears left on the table. I assist in bagging the fresh corn, then I look up and realize we're done! I'm reminded of how much we can accomplish between the five of us (and of course children too).

I leave for home on this hot summer day with ten quart-sized freezer bags of fresh sweet corn. I love the feeling of having "extra" on hand—saving food for the winter is a comforting thought.

A Place at His Table

Denise

"Many hands make light work." I love the picture this saying brings to my mind. Community focused and united toward a specific goal. And the work, sometimes hard, doesn't seem too difficult when we are together talking, laughing, singing, and shifting our minds from the work and onto others.

What does our Lord say about this? He tells us to get busy and get our work done in the season in which we are called. Consider these verses and what they can mean for us as we work together.

> *There is nothing better for a person than that he should eat and drink and find enjoyment in his toil. This also, I saw, is from the hand of God. (Eccles. 2:24 ESV)*

The Lord wants us to find enjoyment while we labor. This satisfaction is granted from God as a simple gift from his hands. He has gifted me with a loving and hardworking family who can work together just as well as we can play together.

> *Six days you shall do you work, but on the seventh you shall rest. (Exod. 23:12 ESV)*

Working and resting have always been important to the Lord. He made that clear to his chosen people early on. After resting on Sunday, I am ready for Monday—how about you? (Shh . . . I get excited about Mondays!)

> *Commit your work to the LORD,*
>   *and your plans will be established. (Prov. 16:3 ESV)*

Do you pray before you start your day, your work, your family projects? When I remember to do that, my mind is more at ease, and I think, *He's got this.*

> *Whatever you do, work heartily, as for the Lord. (Col. 3:23 ESV)*

Do you give it your all? Are you "sold out" for the large task ahead? With a group, it's always good to have a directive from a designated leader so each person knows what's expected of them; this ensures you'll all be on the same page and have the same goal in mind. The goal in front of you may be challenging, but with this united front, you can move forward with the same perspective in mind. Working in community brings great satisfaction.

When our family works with the sweet corn, we feel relieved when it is all picked, shucked, sacked, cooked, cut from the cobs, divided, and placed in the freezer. As we clean up and say our goodbyes, we all feel a strong sense of accomplishment from putting in a hard day's work; we know that when we grab a bag of corn from our freezer for a special meal, we will remember our time together.

Jenny shares: The corn factory is a really big job. We have several stations to do the factory-style work. I enjoy using the electric knife to cut the corn off the cob into a tube pan. The kitchen gets pretty sticky and messy, but it's really fun when we girls are all together accomplishing this big task. The kids love to join in too.

Key Ingredients

Annie

The year after my first baby was born, my mom, Grandma Betty, and I started doing "project Wednesdays." Each Wednesday morning, we gathered at one of our homes, rotating each week. We started with a delicious breakfast, a time of Bible reading and prayer, and then got to work! We'd accomplish a home project that wasn't so fun to do by ourselves but was much more fun to do together. I remember cleaning baseboards, weeding gardens, and painting rooms.

But most of all, I remember talking and laughing and enjoying time with two of my favorite women on earth. I remember sharing concerns with one another and praying together. I remember passing my darling baby between us to keep her content while we reached a goal. And I remember learning so much from my mom and grandma about joyfully keeping a home, cooking, and taking care of a baby.

Plan a Work Day to Accomplish a Goal

What is something you would like to accomplish in your home, in your community, or in your spiritual life? Would working together with some of your favorite people make it more fun and make the burden lighter?

Do you hate washing windows? Ask a friend if she'd like to help you for an hour, and then next week help her for an hour. Be sure to sit down after you're finished with an ice-cold beverage as a reward. Maybe you have more tomatoes than you know what to do with. Have a salsa-making party and send everyone home with some.

How could a group of friends or family impact your community? Could you gather to wash the nursery toys once a month? Perhaps you could organize a group to make meals for a local meal ministry. If coordinating schedules is too difficult, you can still achieve a group goal by individually gathering items for a food or clothing drive, fresh fruit for a homeless shelter, or freezer meals for someone ill in the community—simply assign a pickup and/or delivery person. Prayerfully consider getting your own group project system set up! It will be worth your time and effort and add so much joy to your life.

Meet Goals by Walking alongside Each Other

Spiritual goals can be accomplished with the help of others too. I know that I am much more joyful and motivated to memorize Scripture or complete a Bible reading plan when I have made a goal with family members or friends. And I get my reading assignment done when I know I need to be prepared to discuss a chapter or two at the next book club.

Learn Something New by Trading Skills

I love to bake bread, but I cannot sew a thing. I also love to make homemade salsa, but I couldn't garden to save my life. Ask my mom; she's tried so many times to help me sew and garden, but to no avail! So I love to learn new things from friends who are craftier than I am and who have a greener thumb than I do. When we include our friends in accomplishing a task and then they include us in something else, we can learn to enjoy so many new skills.

Build Character & Knowledge by Including Children

Is it just me, or is it usually easier to just get the job done ourselves than to ask the kids to join in? Sometimes including kids makes a job last twice as long! But I know deep down that kids learn wonderful new skills, gain confidence, and increase in godly character when they are asked to help with chores and projects around the home.

Despite the required extra patience, I do love setting goals for completing bigger seasonal projects together. A few projects we've completed together are

cleaning out the toys before Christmas shopping begins, making freezer meals before the birth of a baby, and detailing the van after a long family car ride. And, of course, their favorite—our annual corn factory at Grandma's house.

My kids feel so great about being part of accomplishing a seeable goal. And I've noticed that they take better care of things when they've been asked to help make improvements. What are some projects in which you could include kids? Organizing the garage? Spring cleaning? Sorting outgrown clothes for donation? Children are often much more capable than we realize.

Apron Application

1. What daily tasks do you have in your life that you can commit to the Lord?

2. What duty or job of yours do you dislike the most? Brainstorm three ways you can make it more enjoyable.

3. Do you remember when you first learned of the value of hard work? Write a few short sentences describing that lesson.

4. When you were younger, did you get to work alongside your parents or grandparents? What are your favorite memories of those times?

5. In what project can you include children in your life? What lesson can you include to help build their character?

Prayer

Heavenly Father, we are thankful for the daily opportunities you give us to learn, work, and grow with others in our lives. We ask that you continue to help guide us in our tasks as we strive to do all things to honor and glorify you. Give us grace and patience to engage and educate those around us, and help keep us focused on the value of hard work and the rewards of joyfully serving you. We commit our work and plans to you, Lord. In Jesus's name we pray, Amen.

Gather at Your Table

Plan ahead and set aside a work day that can be done with a group of those willing to help or teach a new skill. Utilize one another by making your work light. The recipes that follow will allow you to make the meal ahead of time and have hot sandwiches ready when everyone needs a break. Add a tasty drink or dessert that will be sure to reward your guests for their efforts. Don't forget to have fun along the way!

Shirley Temples

12 oz. grenadine, chilled
1 (2 l.) bottle ginger ale, chilled
1 (15 oz.) jar maraschino cherries

Directions

For each 16 oz. glass, pour in 3 Tbs grenadine, then add ginger ale to ⅔ full. Add 2 maraschino cherries and ice to fill. Don't forget the straw!

Note: Stir, if desired; however, this beverage is pretty when not stirred.

Prep time: 5 minutes
Chill time: 4+ hours
Yield: 6 servings

Homemade Ice Cream

2 cups heavy cream
2 cups whole milk
1 cup sugar
3 Tbs vanilla extract
pinch kosher salt

Directions

1. Place all ingredients in a blender; blend until ingredients are completely combined and sugar is dissolved.
2. Pour batter into ice cream maker and follow manufacturer's instructions to freeze the ice cream.
3. Pour ice cream into freezer-safe container, seal, and freeze for at least 4 hours before serving.

Grandma Maxine's Peach Cobbler

Prep time: 15 minutes
Cook time: 35–40 minutes
Yield: 12 servings

8–9	fresh, ripe peaches, blanched, peeled, and sliced
2 Tbs	all-purpose flour
¾ cup	sugar
1 tsp	almond extract

For the topping

2 cups	flour
½ cup	sugar
2 tsp	baking powder
½ cup	margarine or butter, cubed
⅓–½ cup	milk
	sugar for sprinkling

Directions

1. Preheat oven to 350°.
2. Grease a 9x9 baking dish. Place sliced peaches in dish.
3. Mix together flour, sugar, and almond extract. Sprinkle over the peaches.
4. For the topping, combine flour, sugar, and baking powder. Cut in margarine or butter with a pastry blender. Add milk, a little at a time, until batter is moist.
5. Drop topping by the spoonful onto peaches. Sprinkle additional sugar on top.
6. Bake for 35–40 minutes, or until peaches are soft and cobbler is golden brown.

Vegetable Pizza

Prep time: 30 minutes
Cook time: 9 minutes
Yield: 12 servings

4 cups	total assorted raw veggies of your choice, chopped (such as carrots, onions, celery, broccoli, cauliflower, tomatoes)
2 tubes	prepackaged croissant dinner rolls
8 oz.	cream cheese, softened
8 oz.	chip dip (like French or toasted onion) or light sour cream
1 Tbs	dry ranch dressing mix
1½ cups	fancy shredded cheddar cheese (or your preferred cheese)
1 tsp	dill weed

Directions

1. Preheat oven to 350°.
2. Spray large cookie sheet with cooking spray.
3. Unroll croissants and press together on the cookie sheet to make a large crust. Bake for about 9 minutes. Cool completely.
4. Beat together cream cheese, chip dip, and ranch dressing; mix until well combined. Spread on the cooled crust.
5. Add chopped veggies (the smaller the chop, the better they'll stay on each serving).
6. Top with shredded cheese and sprinkle with dill weed. Refrigerate until serving.

Cold Tomato Salad

Prep time: 10 minutes
+ 2–3 hours chill time
Yield: 6–8 servings

6 medium to large tomatoes, cut into eight wedges
1 green pepper, chopped
½ medium onion, chopped
1 cup Italian salad dressing
¼ cup fresh cilantro, chopped (optional)

Directions

1. Place vegetables in medium bowl and mix well. Gently mash down on tomatoes to start juices running.
2. Sprinkle with cilantro, if desired.
3. Toss veggies with salad dressing. Marinate in refrigerator for 2–3 hours.
4. Serve cold in small (clear glass) bowls. It's also fun to serve this salad in a quart or half-gallon jar with a ladle.

— Slow Cooker Italian Beef Sandwiches —

Prep time: 2 minutes
Cook time: 6-8 hours
Yield: 10 servings

2-3 lbs. beef roast
1 (8 oz.) jar pepperoncini (reserve a few for topping, if desired)
½ cup juice from the pepperoncini jar
1 pkg Italian salad dressing mix
10 hoagie buns
shredded or sliced mozzarella cheese, optional

Directions

1. Place the roast in a slow cooker. Top with pepperoncini and pour the juice in the bottom. Pour the Italian dressing packet on top of the roast. Cook on low for 6-8 hours (or overnight).
2. Shred the meat with two forks.
3. Make sandwiches with the hoagie buns, topping with additional pepperoncini and cheese, if desired. Pop under the broiler, open-faced, for about 3 minutes if you'd like a toasty, melty sandwich.
4. Serve with the broth to dip sandwich, if desired.

Fresh Sweet Corn
with Seasoned Butters

Prep time: 5 minutes
+ 2 hours rest time
Cook time: 7 minutes
Yield: 12 servings

1 dozen   full ears fresh sweet corn, shucked

For herb butter

½ cup   salted butter, softened (1 stick)
1 Tbs   fresh parsley, finely chopped
1 Tbs   fresh rosemary, finely chopped
¼ tsp   ground pepper

For cilantro-lime butter

½ cup   butter, softened (1 stick)
¼ cup   fresh cilantro, finely chopped
1–2 cloves   garlic, minced
1 tsp   lime juice
½ tsp   kosher salt

Directions

1. In a medium bowl, combine all of the ingredients for desired butter flavor until evenly combined. Let sit for 2 hours for the herbs to infuse the butter, then stir again and either wrap and refrigerate for later use or use right away.
2. Fill a large stockpot three-fourths full of water and place over high heat. Once water is at a rolling boil, add sweet corn and cook for approximately 7 minutes. Remove ears and let cool slightly.
3. Add butter to hot corn and serve immediately.

   Note: Butters will keep for up to seven days in the fridge.

129

Fall

Hayride, Easy Sunday Supper & Bonfire

*Resting Together
on the Sabbath*

Chili Dogs

Grandma Maxine's Soft Ginger Cookies

Apple Cranberry Coleslaw

Dried Beef Pickle Roll Dip

Fritos Corn Salad

S'mores Buffet

Sunday rest. Doesn't that sound enticing? We work hard, play hard, and long to take a little time off to breathe deeply, enjoy one another, and rejuvenate. When we rest on Sunday, what Christians recognize as "the Lord's day," we turn our eyes away from the weekly grind and look toward relaxation, relationship, and worship. As our family worships at our local church, we refresh spiritually. This "set aside" weekly appointment has become a holy habit and tradition.

On one particular Sunday, our family gathered to sit back, relax, and "smell the cattle." Imagine, if you will, you're along for the bumpy, rural, scenic ride. There's a chill in the air. We decide it's the perfect Sunday afternoon for a family hayride. The air is crisp, and the sun shines bright. Together, for just a few hours, we want to relax and catch up on what's going on in our family's lives as we experience a little fun.

After naptime, here they come. We "load 'em all up and move 'em out." Grandpa lines the lowboy with hay bales for seats. We laugh and sing on the low-to-the-ground trailer as we bump along in the cool, fresh air, enjoying the great outdoors, the closeness of family, and the vivid colors of our autumn countryside.

Then the cows, about thirty of them, come running straight toward us. Fast. They must've spotted the hay bales on the edges of the lowboy and agreed together that they needed an afternoon snack.

My mind starts racing. *Whose idea was this restful pastoral hayride, anyway?* I wasn't really planning on a cattle competition today, just a little quality time relaxing with our family. But the cows are now in hot pursuit! Their fast pace breaks into a trot. A fast trot. Then they're running full speed ahead.

A couple of the "mama jocks" soon catch up to us, not really caring about our seating arrangements. They just want our seats—and by golly, one ol' mama succeeds in pulling a hay bale right off the lowboy! "Giddy up, Grandpa!" I yell to Mr. Farmer. We hang on for dear life as he speeds up his muddy farm truck, until we're finally out of danger. That was a close one.

After our brisk and adventurous ride, it's time to go home. "I've got some chili dogs warming on the stovetop," I announce. The girls each brought a favorite dish to share. We eat together, finishing our supper with Fritos Corn Salad, Apple Cranberry Coleslaw, and Grandma Maxine's Soft Ginger Cookies, fresh from the oven.

Did you enjoy the ride?

After supper, we built a bonfire out back, then helped the children slide marshmallows onto long sticks and brought out graham crackers and chocolate bars for optional traditional (and some nontraditional) s'mores. As the children roasted the sticky sweetness, we all reflected on our time together, seated around the beautiful fiery blaze. We laughed. We listened.

We Sabbathed together.

And what do you suppose our main topic of discussion was? You got it: hungry cows! Maybe next time we'll use different seating.

Jenny shares: Whenever we are outside, our golden retriever, Maggie, is with us. Of course she came along for our hayride and lay at our feet, resting, at the bonfire while we roasted marshmallows. She brings so much joy to the whole family. She loves to show her kindness to all by wanting to play fetch all the time. And when we circle around to visit, there she is, right in the middle.

A Place at His Table

Molly

I *always* look forward to Sunday, because I intentionally set it aside for restoration. Our leisurely hayride was just that—a time to rest and catch up. There have been many occasions when I purposefully work a little harder on Saturday so that Sunday can be an "easy" day for me to spend time in areas I might have missed throughout the week. Sunday has also become my day of "storing up" for the week ahead—both spiritually and physically. For me, this means deeper study and reflection of God's Word and intentionally carving out carefree family time at the farm. This day is important because it prepares me for what may come, and I linger in our relationships just a little bit longer . . .

Setting aside a day of rest can seem easy in theory, right? A day to rest—a day to just do nothing? Okay, well, not exactly that. When we look to the Bible for a better explanation of Sabbath, we find these words in Exodus 20:8–11:

> *Remember the Sabbath day by keeping it holy. Six days you shall labor and do all your work, but the seventh day is a sabbath to the Lord your God. On it you shall not do any work. . . . For in six days the Lord made the heavens and the earth, the sea, and all that is in them, but he rested on the seventh day. Therefore the Lord blessed the Sabbath day and made it holy.*

On the Sabbath day we are to *rest* and *worship*. God asks us to find both physical and spiritual rest.

Physical Rest

We need rest from our labor. Without rest, our bodies can shut down as a means of survival. Our bodies become tired, and without sleep our cognition becomes markedly impaired. Thus, our ability to perform tasks falters. Our physical bodies need a chance to relax, rest, and recover.[1]

Spiritual Rest

Jesus said, "Come to me, all you who are weary and burdened, and I will give you rest. Take my yoke upon you and learn from me, for I am gentle and humble in heart, and you will find rest for your souls. For my yoke is easy and my burden is light" (Matt. 11:28–30). We find peace, and thus spiritual rest, when our hearts and minds are melded in Christ. Friend, has it been an exceptionally tough week? Or even if you've had a fairly basic, smooth week, we all still have everyday struggles and pressures. Think of all the areas that can take our time, energy, and even joy. Jesus will take all of our worries, fears, doubts, and concerns. When we give them to him, we will find perfect peace (Isa. 26:3).

The other half of the meaning of the Sabbath is worship. On the Sabbath day we are called to worship our Lord. What do you think of the word *worship*? For me, I think of going to church and physically worshiping through song and praise. To worship also means to adore or have deep respect.[2] I think of the adoration I have for Christ, and on "his day" I especially desire to please him. I want him to be the entirety of my day—being thankful for all he provides, loving one another, being refreshed and renewed in his presence, and saving up in my heart the moments of today.

Spiritually, God wants us to have a fresh outlook and strength throughout our walk with him—renewing this through continual education and the study of his Word. Romans 12:2 instructs us to "be transformed by the renewing of [our] mind[s]." I understand this renewal as using God's Word for learning and teaching. We must understand the importance of this and practice it in and through our daily living.

Key Ingredients

Annie

Jesus said, "The Sabbath was made for man" (Mark 2:27). Have you ever thought about that? The Sabbath is a gift from God, and we read about the value of taking a rest day many times throughout Scripture. This means that setting aside a day for rest must be a healthy rhythm to include in our weeks. But in this day and age, it is becoming increasingly more difficult to "be still."

Determine to Prioritize a Day of Rest

As much as I love the idea of actually taking a day off each week, making that a reality is somewhat hard to accomplish. Meals still need to be eaten. Children still need care. The house still needs some tending.

But when I do prepare ahead in the week to take the day off on Sunday, I've found that I really look forward to it. When Sunday rolls around, all of the housework is done, some meals have been prepared in advance, and I've got some extra time to relax, visit with family and friends, spend some additional time with God, and really recharge for the upcoming week. I think of this beautiful passage from *The Message* paraphrase of the Bible:

> *Are you tired? Worn out? Burned out on religion? Come to me. Get away with me and you'll recover your life. I'll show you how to take a real rest. Walk with*

me and work with me—watch how I do it. Learn the unforced rhythms of grace.
I won't lay anything heavy or ill-fitting on you. Keep company with me and you'll
learn to live freely and lightly. (Matt. 11:28–30)

I've made the decision to have a regular day of rest. This is an area in which I need to obey the Lord, to accept his invitation to "get away with him," and to prioritize a different kind of day. A quick note: don't feel defeated if you're in a profession that requires working on Sunday. Instead, find another day to rest that works for your schedule. My husband needs to work on some Sundays, so we simply implement these ideas on whatever day he has off in a particular week.

Prepare Ahead for the Day of Rest

A few quick ideas for Saturday evening: lay out your Sunday clothes, give the kids a bath before bed, set the Sunday breakfast table right after you clean up Saturday's dinner, and wrap up any emails or work that needs to be done before going to bed.

Think Ahead about Meals

Something that makes Sunday really restful for me is to take a break from cooking, which also means taking a break from dishes! Something simple I include in my weekly routine is to double up on a recipe earlier in the week. For example, this week we had lasagna on Saturday, so I simply made two pans. Then we had delicious leftovers on Sunday evening that required no work and no extra dishes. During the cold months of fall and winter, we usually eat soup on Sundays, which I prepare earlier in the week. What is something that you are making earlier in the week that can easily be doubled? Think taco meat, a pan of enchiladas, a baked pasta dish, or an egg bake.

And eating out on Sundays can be so fun and relaxing too, can't it? So, how can we make that happen without burdening the family budget? Personally, I am happy to give up a cable subscription or give kids their haircuts at home in order to save a little for eating out. I also try to have some low-cost meals throughout the week (tomato soup, egg salad sandwiches, and bean burritos, for example) that allow us to save from the grocery budget.

Evaluate What Actually Brings Rest & Refreshment to You

Take a minute now to think about the words *rest* and *refreshment*. What comes to mind? If you had nothing else to do today, how would you spend your time in a restful, refreshing way? Would it be reading a book in the hammock? Watching a few extra episodes of a favorite TV show? (My girls and I would definitely answer yes to this question and watch some beloved BBC.) Perhaps a long FaceTime call with your mom, sister, or best friend would really recharge you. Would it be visiting a new museum, spending time in nature, or slowly browsing through a favorite store? Find a way to include these delights.

What are you currently doing on your Sabbath day that could be relegated to another day? Are you grocery shopping? A slight change that I've made this year is to order my groceries online. What a delight it is to simply pull into that pickup spot and have a friendly worker pop those groceries into the trunk. Are you catching up on laundry or housework? Is there a way those tasks could be completed by the evening before instead? My kids see the value in doing a few more chores earlier in the week so that we can spend Sundays resting together.

A category for us all to evaluate is entertaining. If having a houseful of people is energizing and fun for you, then go for it on your Sabbath day! But if that is a draining task, reserve having friends over for another day and make your Sabbath a quiet, restful time with family only. For me, spending time with friends on Sundays is a wonderful way to recharge and have fun, but in order to not take on a lot of extra work, we often meet up at the local scooter park or

at our favorite burger joint. And, of course, our favorite way to spend a Sunday afternoon is at my parents' farm, but we keep meals easy there by cooking hot dogs and s'mores over a bonfire.

Purpose to Take a Break from Worry & Striving

Each week my pastor says that on Sundays we should really rest in the Lord by "casting all of our cares on him." I love this and try to incorporate this idea into my Sundays, and it is powerful.

Are there things in your life that cause worry and stress? I know that spending too much time on social media and managing finances tend to stir up my mind and generate feelings of inadequacy and unrest. So on Sundays I try to take a break from social media by leaving my phone in my purse, and I pay bills on another day of the week.

For me, going to church is a natural way to "set [my mind] on things above" (Col. 3:2). Spending time in God's Word, in worship, and in fellowship with other believers lifts my thoughts off of earthly things and into kingdom thinking. How can we "set [our] minds on things above" at home? I love playing worship music in our house and in the car on Sundays and spending a little extra time in prayer before church. These rhythms help me "be still, and know" that he is God (Ps. 46:10).

Apron Application

1. What is keeping you from resting on the Sabbath?

2. Do you feel you are lacking more in physical or spiritual rest? What is a practical way you can incorporate some much-needed rest?

3. Let's take some action this week. What worry can you cast on the Lord for your Sabbath day? What household tasks can you spend a little more time on during the week to relieve some of your Sunday burden?

4. Evaluate your family's technology usage. Do electronics or social media sites cause any unrest? Try taking a break (if even for a few hours) from technology this Sabbath.

Prayer

Heavenly Father, thank you for your Word and ever constant provision. You know what is best for all of us. Please show us ways we can incorporate rest into the Sabbath this week and every week. We pray that we not only are resting on the Sabbath but also are placing our focus on you—worshiping you and building our relationship with you. In Jesus's name, Amen.

Gather at Your Table

Gathering our family together on a Sunday afternoon to relax and build relationships doesn't really take much effort. The following recipes can be prepared a day or more in advance—as easy as it gets. Whether it's a hayride, backyard barbeque, or game day, our point is to make it simple, relax together, and stay connected.

Chili Dogs

Prep time: 10 minutes
Cook time: 30 minutes
Yield: 8 chili dogs

2 Tbs	olive oil
½ cup	onion, finely chopped
2 Tbs	green pepper, finely chopped
2 lbs.	ground beef
2 Tbs	water
1 (28 oz.)	can chili beans
1 tsp	chili powder
2 (16 oz.)	cans diced tomatoes with green chiles, drained somewhat
dash	hot sauce, optional
8	hot dogs
8	hot dog buns

Optional toppings

shredded cheddar cheese

raw onion, chopped

ketchup and mustard

Directions

1. In a Dutch oven over medium-high heat, heat olive oil and cook onion and green pepper until onion is translucent.
2. Add ground beef and brown well. Add 2 Tbs water to deglaze the pan, scraping the bottom.
3. Add beans, chili powder, and tomatoes. Simmer for 20 minutes. (At this point, you can move chili to slow cooker on low heat, if desired.)
4. Cook hot dogs over open fire, or grill, pan-fry, or boil them.
5. Place hot dogs in buns; add chili and desired toppings.

Grandma Maxine's
Soft Ginger Cookies

Prep time: 15 minutes
Cook time: 12 minutes
Yield: 4 dozen

⅔ cup	vegetable shortening
1½ cups	sugar
¼ cup	molasses
1	egg
2¼ cups	all-purpose flour
2 tsp	baking soda
1 tsp	ground cloves
1 tsp	ground cinnamon
1 tsp	ground ginger
1 tsp	salt

Directions

1. Preheat oven to 350°.
2. Beat together shortening, sugar, molasses, and egg.
3. In a separate bowl, sift together flour, baking soda, cloves, cinnamon, ginger, and salt. Mix into wet ingredients until well combined.
4. Form dough into small balls (about the size of walnuts) and flatten with fork on cookie sheet.
5. Bake for 12 minutes or until lightly browned on the edges. Let cool slightly, then remove from sheet with metal spatula and cool completely on wire rack or waxed paper.

Note: This recipe works well to make ahead. Bake the cookies, cool completely, and then freeze in an airtight container.

Denise shares: This heartwarming recipe is a multigenerational favorite, as I know Maxine's "Mama," as she always referred to her, also called this a favorite of hers! After browsing through several generations of Grandma's recipes, I spotted this time-tested favorite again and again. These cookies have been in our family for well over one hundred years, and we're still devouring them!

Annie shares: These cookies are comforting and homey, just like Grandma Maxine.

Apple Cranberry Coleslaw

2 (11 oz.) bags	coleslaw mix
1 large	gala apple, chopped
1 cup	dried cranberries
1 cup	pecans, chopped
4	green onions, sliced

For the dressing

¾ cup	mayonnaise
¾ cup	sour cream
¼ cup	apple cider vinegar
2 Tbs	honey
½ tsp	salt
	cracked pepper, to taste

Directions

1. Combine coleslaw mix, apple, cranberries, pecans, and onions in a large bowl. Toss until mixed well. Set aside.
2. In a small bowl, combine dressing ingredients and whisk until smooth. Pour three-fourths of dressing into coleslaw and toss until mixed well. Add remaining dressing as desired.
3. Serve right away, or store covered in refrigerator for up to 6 hours.

Prep time: 7-10 minutes
+ 2 hours chill time
Yield: 6-8 servings

Dried Beef Pickle Roll Dip

1 cup	sour cream
8 oz.	cream cheese, softened
1 tsp	onion powder, optional
5 oz.	dried beef, chopped
¼ cup	dill pickles, chopped

Directions

1. Combine sour cream, cream cheese, and onion powder in bowl. Beat until smooth.
2. Stir in dried beef and pickles. Cover and refrigerate for 2 hours before serving.
3. Serve with tortilla chips and/or crackers.

Fritos Corn Salad

Prep time: 10 minutes
Yield: 8–10 servings

2 (15 oz.) cans	whole kernel corn, drained, or 4 cups fresh or frozen sweet corn
2 cups	cheddar cheese, grated
1 cup	mayonnaise
1 cup	green pepper, chopped
½ cup	red onion, finely chopped
1 (10.5 oz.) bag	chili cheese Fritos, coarsely crushed

Directions

1. Mix first 5 ingredients and chill up to 24 hours.
2. Just before serving, stir in the corn chips.

Shelby shares: This recipe came from my mother. She is always willing to try a new recipe, and years ago this salad was one of those experiments. It's now become a staple recipe for this family and is used for many occasions and gatherings.

S'mores Buffet

Prep time: 5 minutes
Cook time: 3 minutes
Yield: 1–2 per guest

Our s'mores buffet uses a variety of ingredients for some truly unique s'mores. Let your imagination run wild, and gather all of your friends' favorite cookies and candy! Make sure to grab enough ingredients that everyone can have at least two different s'mores.

Outer ingredients

graham crackers
Keebler Fudge Stripe cookies
Keebler Coconut Dreams cookies
Ritz crackers
gluten-free almond or sugar cookies

Filling ingredients

chocolate bars
marshmallows
Caramello bars
peanut butter cups
strawberry marshmallows

The Pumpkin Patch

*Bringing Generations Together
through Tradition*

Harvest Snack Mix

Homemade Granola Bars

Popcorn Munch

Cinnamon Sugar Pecans

Shelby ————

Our family has established an "accidental" autumn tradition. It started on a whim when one of us extended the invitation to meet at a local pumpkin patch. Grandparents, parents, and grandchildren all joined together to enjoy the seasonal activities, and we had such a good time we couldn't wait to do it again. We look forward to it each year; we pack the guys' coolers as they head back to the fields and then load up our bags, strollers, and snacks. And away we go, each car filled with excitement and members of multiple generations.

This warm fall afternoon was spent together at the pumpkin patch among a backdrop of vibrant fall leaves, bright orange pumpkins, and little heads bobbing around rows of giant mums. This event has grown to include all of our families. Along with us Gingham Apron gals and our children, my mother, Lorilyn, and Molly's mother, Cath, have joined as well, blending all of our families for an afternoon. Once we arrive it's a blur of kids running from one activity to the next—riding ponies, picking out pumpkins, and feeding farm animals. Cameras flash, grandmas beam, and grandkids chatter and ask question after question, sparking joy for the adults with their great curiosity and large imaginations.

We anticipate and wait patiently for the tractor to pick us up for the hayride that will take us way out back to the field that contains the prize pumpkins each kid will choose, and memories are sparked as if it were yesterday of Grandma taking a ride on her daddy's tractor and going to pick up square hay bales, and she shares her story with the children as we ride back to the farmyard.

We eventually gather to have our snacks, and while the kids chatter and giggle, we reflect on what this past year has given us. Traditions, accidental or not, have an amazing ability to connect us, comfort us, and give us a feeling of collective identity. Sure, the little kids see the annual trip to the pumpkin patch as just a fun time to run around with their cousins, but I see it as something greater.

There is much to be gained by gathering with those of different generations. When I think of older generations, I cherish the wisdom and life experiences they can share. Those a generation younger than me can also offer a different perspective and a refreshing energy. One of the most valuable aspects one generation can pass to another is their faith, through sharing their stories of how God has led them and blessed them through the years.

> *One generation commends your works to another;*
>   *they tell of your mighty acts.*
> *They speak of the glorious splendor of your majesty—*
>   *and I will meditate on your wonderful works.*
> *They tell of the power of your awesome works—*
>   *and I will proclaim your great deeds.*
> *They celebrate your abundant goodness*
>   *and joyfully sing of your righteousness. (Ps. 145:4–7)*

A Place at His Table

Denise

Bubbling over with excitement, we all play in the corn pile and then watch the children frolic at the farm-themed playground. We giggle and laugh as we bite into a caramel apple or open wide for another handful of kettle corn.

Grandkids and grandmas, mothers and daughters. We listen and share as we meander through the pumpkins and ponies, goats and gourds, reminiscing about grandmas gathering the pumpkins and gourds from their garden and helping their parents weed and pick from their own patch. The children love to hear the stories of past generations on the farm.

We also talk about the beauty of the earth and the gathering of produce in harvest. We view God's creatures close-up as we feed the goats and ride the ponies. We are reminded of Psalm 104, which is a perfect devotion when in the great outdoors. "How many are your works, Lord! In wisdom you made them all; the earth is full of your creatures" (v. 24). Together, our faith in Christ grows.

With each generation comes change. Machines and technology continue to bring the farmer greater ease to long hours of work. When my father-in-law started farming, it was with a team of horses, for example. But some things never change. The beauty of the earth with its four seasons in the heartland never changes. Springtime and harvest will come and go until the end. To look forward to and celebrate these yearly milestones with our loved ones is such a treat.

Walking along with the children and grandchildren is a perfect time for us to talk about loving the Lord and his creation. It's also a perfect time to show the love of God to each other as we sit and walk and ride and listen along—right in the middle of autumn's treasure chest. Promises like this one from God's Word make reading it such a treasure:

> *Your children will be like olive shoots*
> *around your table.*
> *Behold, thus shall the man be blessed*
> *who fears the Lord. (Ps. 128:3–4 ESV)*

As we gather for our snack time, we praise God for his bountiful harvest once again. We share our joys and sorrows, our prayer requests and praises, and our answered prayers. We talk about where we see God at work. We include the children as we thank God for this beautiful day and our time together.

Let the message of Christ dwell among you richly as you teach and admonish one another with all wisdom through psalms, hymns, and songs from the Spirit, singing to God with gratitude in your hearts. (Col. 3:16)

We value our time together, our time with the children and our time with each generation that enriches our lives. This is a priority to us. It doesn't just happen. We must act and make it happen. Include the children in planning the date for the next outing—to the pumpkin patch or whatever other tradition you have. Keep it going.

Who knows? You may just get an invite to help carve the prize pumpkin!

Key Ingredients

Purposefully Pair the Old & Young

There is something really special and unique about the "older generation" and the "younger generation." Have you noticed how grandmas and grandpas light up when a young person is around them? It's wonderful to be intentional about inviting a grandparent or someone special to outings such as going to the pumpkin patch, getting ice cream, attending a grandparents' lunch, going to a play or musical, or even simply telling stories together and looking through old photos.

Visit a Local Nursing Home

Every year my children come with me to deliver poinsettias from our church to our local nursing home, and I always come away astounded from our trip because these mature folks are so tickled to see young children frolicking about. Sometimes I wonder if they have forgotten what it was like to be a kid and this gives them an opportunity to feel joy resonating with that memory once again. When it's time for us to leave, the nursing home folks have grins on their faces from ear to ear.

Treasure a New Skill Together

When I reflect back on memories of my own childhood, I can think of specific instances when I learned from my late grandfather. My grand "Fa" as we called him had a love and passion for many skills in life, and one thing he taught me was how to fish. I learned how to cast and bait a hook in fresh water and salt water, and I even think I learned patience (at least some) from fishing. The skills I learned and memories I have will remain with me forever.

Pass on Faith

Often it's a grandparent or parent who first shares with us about their faith. For others, it may be a dear friend or someone else who simply desires to intimately share their faith. Whatever the circumstance, one of the best ways to learn is from those who are older—or in some cases younger—than us. It may be through deliberate instruction or teaching, or simply through modeling by example. Host a church gathering specifically for the purpose of bringing generations together; this could be through a unique gathering or by connecting different Bible study groups, for example.

Utilize Your Childlike Wonder

Have you ever thought what it would be like to be a kid again? Sure, we all have those thoughts now and then. But have you ever just allowed yourself to be vulnerable and "discover" again? Although I can't go back in time, I can try to engage in a seasonal craft, a scavenger hunt, baking, or simply building a LEGO castle with my kids. This unravels my imagination, and I find myself having just as much fun as they are.

Apron Application

Annie

1. How can you share your heritage with your children or other family members or friends? Plan a time to share a family story so it can continue to be passed down. Something I wish I'd done before losing my grandmas was to "interview" them about specific times in their lives.

2. How can you add more generational variety to your life? Can you join a church small group that is organized by location instead of age demographics? Can you ask an older woman over for coffee or to mentor you? Ask God how.

3. How can you honor an older, special family member? Perhaps it's time to write a letter telling a parent or grandparent how special they are to you or to recall a special time you had together.

Prayer

Heavenly Father, thank you for how you have created families with multiple generations who can encourage, teach, and strengthen one another. Help us treasure the gifts of grandparents and parents. Show us how to enrich our lives by spending time with people from different generations. Give us the courage to reach out to someone older or younger than us so that we may grow in our knowledge of you. In Jesus's name, Amen.

Gather at Your Table

For this outdoor fall gathering, we tried to keep it simple. We packed tasty snacks, some of which included seasonal ingredients such as candy corn and fall-colored M&Ms, to eat on the go while picking out pumpkins. You can find yourself a picnic table or hay bales, or bring along a blanket. The natural beauty of the changing leaves provides a beautiful backdrop for any outdoor gathering, requiring no added decor and allowing us to focus more on our time together.

Harvest Snack Mix

Prep time: 5 minutes
Cook time: 40 minutes
Yield: 20–24 servings

1½ cups	butter, melted (3 sticks)
1½ cups	brown sugar
3 Tbs	vanilla extract
1 (12 oz.) box	Rice Chex cereal
1 (7 oz.) bag	Bugles
3 cups	mini pretzels
1 cup	Brach's Autumn Mix (or a blend of candy corn and candy pumpkins)
1 (8 oz.) bag	Reese's Pieces

Directions

1. Preheat oven to 275°.
2. Combine melted butter, brown sugar, and vanilla and whisk well.
3. In a very large bowl or brown paper bag, add Chex, Bugles, and pretzels, and stir gently until combined. Pour butter mixture over cereal and toss gently until evenly coated.
4. Line two large cookie sheets with parchment paper. Divide mixture between both sheets and spread out into an even layer. Bake for 40 minutes, stirring every 10–15 minutes.
5. Remove from oven and let cool.
6. Return to large bowl and add candy corn/pumpkin mix and Reese's Pieces. Gently toss to combine.
7. Store in an airtight container.

Homemade Granola Bars

Prep time: 15 minutes
Cook time: 35–40 minutes
Yield: 12 servings

3 cups	rolled oats
1 cup	sliced almonds
½ cup	toasted wheat germ
2 Tbs	ground flax seed (optional)
3 Tbs	unsalted butter
⅔ cup	honey
¼ cup	light brown sugar, lightly packed
1½ tsp	pure vanilla extract
¼ tsp	kosher salt
1½ cups	dried cranberries

Directions

1. Preheat oven to 350°. Butter an 8x12 baking dish and line with parchment paper. Set aside.
2. Toss oats and almonds together on a sheet pan. Bake for 10–12 minutes, stirring occasionally, until lightly browned. Transfer to a large mixing bowl and stir in wheat germ and optional ground flax seed.
3. Reduce oven temperature to 300°.
4. Place butter, honey, brown sugar, vanilla, and salt in a small saucepan and bring to a boil over medium heat. Cook and stir for 1 minute, then pour over the toasted oats mixture. Add cranberries and stir well.
5. Pour mixture into prepared pan. Wet your fingers and lightly press mixture evenly into the pan. Bake for 25–30 minutes, until light golden brown. Cool for at least 2 hours before cutting into squares. Serve at room temperature.

Popcorn Munch

Prep time: 5 minutes
Cook time: 2–5 minutes
to pop popcorn
Yield: 20–24 servings

16–20 cups   popped popcorn (or 2 bags plain microwave popcorn)
1 lb.   white/vanilla almond bark

Optional ingredients

1–2 cups   fall-colored M&Ms
Reese's Pieces
fall-colored sprinkles

Directions

1. Place popped popcorn in a very large bowl or brown paper bag, removing any unpopped kernels.
2. Break up almond bark and melt according to package directions. Pour over popcorn and stir well.
3. Add optional ingredients as desired and continue to stir until everything is well coated. Spread onto waxed paper or parchment paper to cool completely. Once cool and dry, break up into clumps.
4. Store in airtight container for up to a week.

Shelby shares: This was a favorite snack when visiting my Grandma Esther growing up. It is a favorite of my kids as well. We have it around for birthdays, holidays, and game nights. Just change up the optional ingredients to fit your special occasion!

Cinnamon Sugar Pecans

Prep time: 5 minutes
Cook time: 1 hour
Yield: 12 servings

1 cup   sugar
2 tsp   ground cinnamon
1 tsp   salt
     2   egg whites, beaten
2 Tbs   water
½ tsp   vanilla
16 oz. pecan halves

Directions

1. Preheat oven to 250°. Line a baking sheet with parchment paper and set aside.
2. In a large bowl, mix together sugar, cinnamon, and salt. Set aside.
3. In separate bowl, whisk together egg whites, water, and vanilla. Slowly stir in pecans until well coated. With a slotted spoon, remove pecans and place in the cinnamon sugar mix. Gently stir until evenly coated.
4. Spoon pecans onto parchment-lined baking sheet in a single, even layer. Bake for 1 hour, stirring and shaking pan every 15 minutes.

A Real Tailgating Party

Encouraging Those in Your Life

Spiced Apple Cider

Cheesy Mac & Corn

Grandma Betty's Potato Salad

Calico Beans

Sloppy Joe Sliders

Snickerdoodles

Oh Henry! Bars

Shelby ————

For most of us, fall tends to be an extremely busy time of the year, with kids getting back to school, changing routines, and weekly schedules to fulfill. Fall is also an especially busy time for our husbands—our farmers who work countless hours to get the harvest completed while the weather is favorable. There is great urgency to get the soybeans and corn picked from the fields before they get too dry and before the weather turns cold and snowy. We knew that we wanted one of our fall gatherings to really show them we saw how hard they were working.

As farmers' wives, we can feel as though there is a lot on our shoulders to sustain the family amid the running combines. The days are long for us too—having supper ready and then getting to homework and activities, shuttling kids, picking up the slack from a hardworking husband who's in the fields, and then preparing to do it all over the next day. Conversations with our men are limited and prove to be challenging while they are working away in the combine and communicating through the constant equipment noise. We knew all of us could benefit from drawing together as a family during such a busy and stressful time.

Since there is no stopping the men until they are finished, we cannot expect them to take the time to come in for a nourishing, warm meal, so we decided to have a tailgate picnic. This meal would be a much-needed pause to celebrate together on a typical harvest day. The men were worn out and could definitely use a little pick-me-up, plus they were getting tired of having cold sandwiches for lunch and supper most days. By gathering in the field, we could meet them where they were, and we too could absorb the autumn sights and smells that undoubtedly provide a backdrop of encouragement for us all. The brown, dried-up corn stalks and shades of golden rolling hills against the gray hazy sky reminded us of God's bounty and goodness.

Molly

It's late afternoon on this warm fall day, with heat and excitement swirling around us, and as our fleet of four vehicles hits the gravel road, dust rapidly encompasses us. The guys have been harvesting for over a month. The soybeans are finished, and they are on to the corn. We can't wait to surprise them with this tangible encouragement to keep going.

Our fleet arrives at the rendezvous point, a cornfield, and we realize it is becoming quite windy. Fortunately, the cornstalks provide a natural wind barrier for our picnic. The sky is getting darker as we lay out our spread of food along a tailgate. Our menu of Sloppy Joe Sliders, Grandma Betty's Potato Salad, Calico Beans, and Cheesy Mac & Corn smell and look comforting to everyone, and we know the men will be thrilled to have a warm meal brought to them. The children have already spotted the desserts: Oh Henry! Bars and Snickerdoodles. Soon comes one combine, then another, and then the tractor and grain cart, signaling that the men are coming in.

This hearty meal hopefully speaks to the guys, "We are with you. We care about you and we see you working hard." We know that sometimes their work can go unnoticed by us or our children. One day is just like the next. How can we encourage them with our words, and how can we celebrate them? Today it's by rolling out their favorites so that they can say in their hearts, *They see us*.

We're all together in the cornfield. Children are playing and anticipating getting a ride on a combine. It's a fun, relaxing evening, and we're grateful to spend time together with the people we love. It's in this deep love of the things God has given us that we realize he encourages us so that we can encourage others.

For us, sometimes encouragement looks like not only meal planning but actually taking the meal to others. We carefully planned the menu for today. It was especially important to choose hearty, warm, comforting dishes that would show our guys how much we appreciated their hard work.

Our original real tailgating party was several years ago, and it has now become an annual, much-anticipated event for our extended farm family, where everyone (including us) leaves feeling appreciated, encouraged, and refreshed.

A Place at His Table

Denise

Our real tailgating parties have caused us to reflect upon how we can encourage those in our life. What well can we draw deeply from to get our example of encouragement? The story of Barnabas is a wonderful place to begin. Did you know the apostles actually named him? The close followers of Jesus saw something intriguing in their new brother, Joseph, and began calling him by the name Barnabas, which means "the son of encouragement." I love that.

Barnabas was "sold out" for Jesus and did many acts of encouragement. When he became a Christian, he was a landowner. He put his faith into action and sold his piece of land, laying the money at the apostles' feet to be used for spreading the gospel (Acts 4:36–37). He then saw other needs to fill, and off he went. What an encouragement that must have been for his newfound brothers and sisters in Christ.

Barnabas was willing to help, made himself available, and jumped at the chance to serve obediently in whatever tasks were laid before him. He even introduced Paul, as a new convert, to his brothers in Jerusalem (9:26–30). I long to be like Barnabas. When I read his story, I crave to do a better job for Jesus, to reach out with encouraging words and kindness and lovingly help others along in their faith. This man was also an *adventurer* for God. He taught, he encouraged others in their faith, and he didn't stop. He fulfilled missions in one town and journeyed on to the next, always ready for a chance to serve. The Bible says Barnabas was "a good man, full of the Holy Spirit," and he did the Lord's bidding wherever he went (11:24).

Let's be like Barnabas in our marriages, our families, our homes, our churches, our communities, and our mission fields . . . wherever the Lord leads us.

Key Ingredients

Annie

Encouraging others isn't hard, is it? We all need encouragement in every season of life—a kind word, a hand that reaches out when we need to be *seen*. How can we show encouragement to those around us? When making a delicious dish, we need a recipe with just the right ingredients. In the same way, encouraging others takes a plan with some fitting ingredients.

Share Heirloom Treasures

As we've mentioned, one of our favorite ways to add meaning to a gathering is to use some family heirloom recipes. We've found that recipes like these help us fondly remember special people and occasions. Do you have a favorite family recipe you can prepare for family or friends? The next time you share that dish, take a minute to tell your group about where that recipe came from and how special it is to you. And then ask others the question, "What is a favorite family recipe of yours?"

Instead of a recipe, you can also bring other types of family history to a gathering, such as an heirloom quilt to sit on or another item or a picture—whatever can add richness to the event! We can encourage someone by talking with them about their favorite family heirlooms. How is that encouraging? You are showing others that you see them, and you are drawing out of them something of value. And when others perceive that you see value in them or what they have to offer, you have already encouraged them more than you know.

Check Off Others' Bucket Lists

We've enjoyed a lighthearted version of checking items off a bucket list with our family. Our bucket lists are seasonal or holiday-themed and include the best of each season. We love making a fall bucket list, posting it on the fridge, and then checking off as many events as we can throughout that season. What might be on a friend's seasonal bucket list? Or someone who especially needs some encouragement? In planning your own gathering to encourage others, consider an event that centers on an item on their list. Here are a few ideas:

Enjoy apple cider together on the porch or around a firepit.

Jump in a pile of leaves.

Take a hayride at a local farm.

Take photos in a park filled with fall colors.

Go horseback riding.

Go on a nature walk, gathering treasures as you go.

Visit a local hiking area to take in the foliage from a new height.

Take kids to a pumpkin patch.

Make autumn-themed cutout cookies.

Here's the beauty of bucket lists: you can include so many different people! Family, friends, neighbors, and church groups can all join an activity you've planned for this season.

Include Children in Encouraging Loved Ones

My sisters-in-law and I love involving our kids in practices that build others up. Recently my husband celebrated his thirty-seventh birthday, so my kids made illustrated posters—thirty-seven of them—that each listed one thing they loved about their daddy. Then, when he came home from work, they were excited to show him the posters that filled a whole wall. Some posters focused on the less important things in life—"You're really handsome!" "You know all the names of the cars!" But other cards were tearjerkers—"Thank you for always taking us to church and for teaching us about God." "Thank you for working so hard for our family." He *loved* it! I know we made his birthday really special.

If you have kids, consider asking them to make homemade invitations to a special family or friend gathering you're planning. Our kids once mailed handmade invites to Grandpa and Grandma for a "restaurant night" at our house. Kids love to be involved, and adults love to receive a special handwritten, words-misspelled, smudged, construction-paper invitation. You better believe that Grandpa and Grandma were excited to come and order off those hand-made menus.

Make a Craft

Making a craft can be both encouraging and memorable. Think of something that you know your guests will enjoy, even if it's simple. Whenever your guests see that craft in their home, their minds will be flooded with warm memories of the time spent with you and others. My daughter gathered a few friends together last year for a fall party, and they made yarn pumpkins that each took home. Other fall ideas include pinecone bird feeders, leaf rubbings (for little ones), or a leaf wreath.

Broaden the Circle

Sometimes being encouraging means getting outside our comfort zones of family and friends. Have you considered baking an apple pie for a struggling neighbor, coworker, or fellow church member? How about taking the kids to an elderly neighbor's yard to rake leaves? How can you connect with people in your life? Maybe your meeting place isn't a cornfield but a quaint little park a few blocks away. Or why not organize a neighborhood tailgating party in your driveway? My Bible study leader recently hosted a pizza night for our group. She simply picked up the pizza and dessert but set her table

in a beautiful, feminine theme with paper plates and napkins. It was simple yet wonderful, and encouraging for all who came because they felt seen, heard, and wanted.

Apron Application

Denise

1. Hebrews 3:13 calls us to "encourage one another daily, as long as it is called 'Today.'" Notice that this verse says *today*. Today, think about someone in your life who could use some encouragement. Who around you is struggling, lonely, tired, or simply needs to be noticed? What is one action you can take to build him or her up?

2. When you intentionally encourage others, what do you discover in the process? What is God giving you in your heart as you reach out to others?

3. What are some unique gathering ideas that would strengthen those in your life?

Prayer

Dear Jesus, my desire is to become an encourager to those around me. Show me ways to build strong relationships not just within my family but in the lives of any others you put before me. I know that you bring each person into my life for a purpose. Guide me to love others, to be a light, and to point others to you. Provide me with clarity to see those who need encouragement. In Jesus's name I pray, Amen.

Gather at Your Table

With this rustic fall setting and our large group of people, we selected favorite recipes that were easy to serve to our crew while on the go. The children equally relished this outdoor tailgate event, and it has become a lasting tradition we all look forward to during the busy season of harvest.

Spiced Apple Cider

1 gal.	apple cider
2 Tbs	red hot candies
1	orange, thinly sliced
2	apples, cored and quartered
5	cinnamon sticks
1 Tbs	whole cloves

Prep time: 5 minutes
Cook time: 30 minutes
Yield: 16 (8 oz.) servings

Directions

1. Place all ingredients in a large saucepan.
2. Heat over medium-low, stirring occasionally, until the cider is warm and the red hots have dissolved completely. Discard oranges, apples, cinnamon sticks, and whole cloves before serving.

   Note: This recipe can also be made in the slow cooker by heating all ingredients on low for 8 hours.

Cheesy Mac & Corn

1 (15 oz.) can	whole kernel corn, undrained
1 (15 oz.) can	creamed corn
1 cup	elbow macaroni, uncooked
½ cup	butter, softened (1 stick)
1 cup	Velveeta cheese, cubed

Prep time: 5 minutes
Cook time: 60 minutes
Yield: 8-10 servings

Directions

1. Preheat oven to 375°.
2. Mix together all ingredients in a greased, large casserole dish.
3. Bake, covered with foil, for 30 minutes; uncover and bake for an additional 30 minutes.
4. Stir and serve.

Shelby shares: As a child I would frequently request my mom make this dish. This recipe is easy to make and has the mac & cheese addition that all kids love (even us grown kids).

Grandma Betty's Potato Salad

Prep time: 20 minutes
Cook time: 20–30 minutes
Yield: 8 servings

8–10	white potatoes, peeled and halved or quartered (depending on size), approx. 6 cups
1½–2 cups	mayonnaise
1 tsp	dry mustard
1 tsp	sugar
pinch	pepper
½ cup	onion, diced
6–8	hard-boiled eggs, chopped

Directions

1. Boil potatoes in water (add a pinch of salt) for 20–30 minutes (depending on size of potatoes), until easily pierced with a fork but not so soft they break easily.
2. Rinse, drain, and cool potatoes.
3. In a large bowl, mix together mayonnaise, mustard, sugar, pepper, and onion.
4. Dice potatoes into fairly small pieces.
5. Add potatoes and hard-boiled eggs to mayonnaise mixture. Mix well.
6. Add more mayonnaise if needed. There should be enough mayonnaise to hold it all together. Refrigerate until ready to serve.

Molly shares: As I woke early one Saturday morning to immediately begin cutting the potatoes for Grandma Betty's Potato Salad, I couldn't help but think of all the times she had made her famous salad for parties, picnics, and barbeques, even in her old age. To accommodate different taste preferences, she made not only one but often two—or sometimes even *three*—different varieties. The potatoes were always cut into small, perfect pieces, the onion was diced so finely you could not even tell it was there, and there was always "enough mayonnaise to hold it all together."

We received a phone call at 7:30 a.m. that morning letting us know she was finally home. Her pain and suffering were gone, and she was with the Almighty One. I knew the Holy Spirit was guiding me at that very moment, and that was why I'd woken up early on that particular day to get started on the potato salad. What an honor and a privilege. As I finished dicing the eggs, I felt as though she were whispering the steps to me.

Annie shares: Each time I make this potato salad, I follow the handwritten directions in my "Family Treasured Recipes" book that Grandma Betty made for me as a wedding present. At the bottom of the page, underneath the recipe, there is a note. It reads, "This is the potato salad recipe used at your mom and dad's wedding rehearsal dinner." Grandma Betty was such an encouraging woman. She had endless joy because of her relationship with Jesus.

Calico Beans

Prep time: 10 minutes
Cook time: 1–2 hours
Yield: 14–16 servings

1 lb.	ground beef
½ lb.	bacon, cut up
1	small onion, diced
1 rounded tsp	prepared mustard
2 tsp	vinegar
½ cup	sugar
½ cup	brown sugar
½ cup	ketchup
1 (15 oz.) can	butter beans, drained
1 (15 oz.) can	lima beans, drained
1 (15 oz.) can	kidney beans, drained
1 (15 oz.) can	pork and beans, not drained

Directions

1. Brown ground beef, bacon, and onion in large pot or Dutch oven.
2. Add mustard, vinegar, sugar, brown sugar, and ketchup, and give it a good stir.
3. Add all the beans. Let simmer on stovetop or transfer to oven at 250° for an hour or so, or transfer to slow cooker and let simmer.

Sloppy Joe Sliders

Prep time: 10 minutes
Cook time: 5–10 minutes
Yield: 15 small sandwiches

2 lbs. ground beef
½ onion, chopped or minced according to preference
1 (10.5 oz.) can condensed cream of chicken soup
4 oz. chip dip (toasted onion or French onion flavor)
3 Tbs Heinz 57 sauce
15 artisan buns
cheese slices, optional

Directions

1. Brown ground beef and chopped onion in large skillet; rinse and drain of grease and return to skillet.
2. Add condensed soup, chip dip, and sauce. Combine well, then simmer for 5–10 minutes.
3. Serve on buns, with a slice of cheese, if desired.

Prep time: 15 minutes
Cook time: 9–11 minutes
Yield: 3 dozen

Snickerdoodles

½ cup	vegetable shortening
½ cup	butter, softened (1 stick)
1½ cups	sugar
2	eggs
2¾ cups	all-purpose flour
2 tsp	cream of tartar
1 tsp	baking soda
¼ tsp	salt

Mixture for rolling

3 Tbs	sugar
3 tsp	ground cinnamon

Directions

1. Preheat oven to 375°.
2. In a stand mixer or with a hand mixer, beat together shortening, butter, 1½ cups sugar, and eggs.
3. In a separate bowl, sift together flour, cream of tartar, baking soda, and salt. Add to wet ingredients and mix together on medium-low just until well combined.
4. Mix 3 Tbs sugar and 3 tsp cinnamon together in a small, deep bowl.
5. Form dough into balls about the size of a black walnut. Roll each in cinnamon sugar and place on cookie sheet an inch apart.
6. Bake for 9–11 minutes or until very lightly browned.

Oh Henry! Bars

Prep time: 20 minutes
Cook time: 10 minutes
Yield: 16 servings

¾ cup	butter, softened and divided (1½ sticks)
⅔ cup	brown sugar
2	eggs
2 tsp	vanilla, divided
1½ cups	all-purpose flour
½ tsp	baking powder
¼ tsp	baking soda
3 cups	mini marshmallows
⅔ cup	corn syrup
1 (12 oz.) pkg.	peanut butter chips
2 cups	crisp rice cereal or cornflakes
2 cups	salted peanuts

Directions

1. Preheat oven to 350°.
2. For the first layer, mix ½ cup butter, brown sugar, eggs, 1 tsp vanilla, flour, baking powder, and baking soda together until well combined and place in a greased 9x13 pan. Bake for 8–9 minutes.
3. For the second layer, sprinkle mini marshmallows evenly on top of the first layer. Bake for 1 minute or until marshmallows melt.
4. For the third layer, heat in large pan on stovetop: corn syrup, remaining 1 tsp vanilla, ¼ cup butter, and peanut butter chips until just melted. Remove from heat. Add cereal and peanuts and mix well.
5. Spread cereal mixture over marshmallows. (We recommend greasing your hands to press this layer onto the marshmallows, as it gets pretty sticky.)
6. Cool, slice into bars, and serve.

Winter

Friday Night Pizza Party

Rejoicing in Simple Joys

Blueberry & Strawberry Italian Sodas

Italian Salad

Cheese Bread

Antipasto Platter

Homemade Pizza Dough

Chicken Alfredo Pizza

Margherita Pizza

Hamburger Pizza

Mocha Brownie Torte

Cinnamon Streusel Dessert Pizza

The Friday night pizza party has been around as long as I can remember—even before I joined the Herrick family. When my husband and his siblings were children, they had a Friday night pizza party of their own. It involved pizza, pop, movies, picnic blankets on the floor, and quality family time. It was a special night. For a busy farm family, it was an assurance and comfort to know they could count on everyone being home for a relaxing meal together.

When my husband and I were dating, we would meet up with his family often for pizza, pop, and movies. It was something I always looked forward to. My sister-in-law Annie's kiddos were very little. We loved doting on them—reading books together and playing games. Early in our relationship, this pizza night was planted in my mind as an idea for my own family someday. I enjoyed it so much because I felt like we had created a wholesome, fun-loving atmosphere and were taking the time to enjoy the fruit of refreshment.

Now, as a mother, I love pizza night even more—a night each week we try to intentionally leave open. My kids appreciate it as much as I do. We can set aside our busyness for the night and relax and recover from a bustling week of school, deadlines, extracurricular activities, tests to study for—and, well, you get the picture. On Friday night, we recharge and delight as a family.

Twelve years ago, when I was studying abroad in Rome, Italy, I had some of the most amazing pizza in the world. It could be found on almost every block and would be folded up in a white-lined paper and handed to me in just a few minutes. I was inspired by the refreshing ingredients.

But even more than their pizza, I adored how the Italian people used food and gathering as a staple in their lifestyle. Meals are a top priority for them, and so is taking the time to linger and savor.

During these winter months, we have to get a little more creative about our gatherings. Most of our time is typically spent indoors. For this month's setting, we decided to take our pizza night to the next level between our four families; we created a menu with all of our favorite pizzas, including cheese bread and dessert pizza. We each chose a homemade pizza to contribute, and I decided to

bring some of my experiences from Italy into the pizza making by incorporating fresh ingredients and using a pizza stone, which makes such a difference. For the drinks, we thought this would be the perfect time to introduce a new recipe to our family, Italian sodas. With this recipe we made a simple syrup by heating fruit—such as strawberries and blueberries—and adding a little sugar to it. Then we merely added club soda and a dash of cream.

When we shook out our red-and-white checked tablecloth in Denise's kitchen, we had a snapshot of Italy before us. The table was loaded with bubbled-up, cheesy pizzas. Fresh tomatoes gleamed and mozzarella dripped over the sides of the pans, and the air smelled delightfully of garlic and seasonings. Some of the homemade crusts were thin and bubbly, others thick and hearty. A hefty wooden bowl was filled to the brim with salad. Annie's dessert pizzas captured the eyes of all the children.

After a heavy week of work, meetings, deadlines, loading up cattle, and the general busyness of life, each of us was eager to celebrate and enjoy a lighthearted evening with our own version of "Little Italy." The kids were soon dashing down to the basement, ready to start rummaging through the favorite toy collection at Grandpa and Grandma's, and we were ready to indulge in an evening of refreshment. Our hard work during the week pays off, as moments like this help us understand God's purpose of being able to authentically rejoice together. The work is worth it, and it's in these moments we can comprehend the value of this reward.

A Place at His Table

Annie

On the surface, eating pizza every Friday night might not seem very significant, but for our family it has become a comforting delight. Whether simple or sophisticated, celebrations are important. They seem to convey that though the world can be dark and difficult, and life is hard, we have so much for which to thank God. Celebrations reinforce the fact that our good God is in control and he is blessing us.

Sometimes we need to praise God in recognition of an achievement, a goal met, or even the end of a difficult season. Choosing to rejoice recognizes that he has provided the strength to get the job done or to conquer a difficult time of life.

Sometimes we need to rejoice simply because that's what God has called us to do, and it is so good for us! And we always need to rejoice just because of who God is.

> *This is the day that the Lord has made;*
> *let us rejoice and be glad in it.* (Ps. 118:24 ESV)

One of my favorite joy-filled stories in the Bible is the story of King David "[dancing] before the Lord with all his might" (2 Sam. 6:14). I love that, for a time, David put aside the burdens he carried as the king of a nation at war. And he simply showed God his appreciation and joy by dancing behind the ark of the covenant.

Jesus loved to celebrate! His first recorded miracle took place while he attended a wedding at Cana. And he said, "I have come that they may have life, and have it to the full" (John 10:10).

So let's obey God. Let's rejoice because of who he is and because of the work Jesus has done for each of us on the cross. Let's rejoice because we know he cares for us and loves us well. Let's rejoice when he has helped us come through a hardship or difficult season or accomplish something important.

Key Ingredients

Shelby

When you think of the word *celebration*, what comes to mind? My mind instantly goes to balloons, confetti, cake—some event that is grand and entertaining. But in reality, a celebration doesn't have to be elaborate or expensive at all. It doesn't even have to include a single balloon.

Modeling to our family what we value is important to us. We want everyone to be seen, be heard, and feel connected with one another. We desire to focus on the joys of life, both big and small, and build connections with one another. Celebrating our everyday joys as a family gives all of us a sense of belonging and value and draws us closer to each other.

We celebrated the end of a busy week by "welcoming the weekend" and gathering together to have a simple pizza party; with a little imagination and creativity, you can turn your ordinary days into something to celebrate as well.

Reward Accomplishments

Likewise, our accomplishments do not have to be remarkable or magnificent for us to praise them. When we are not clouded by the daily struggles of life, we can focus on each other's simple accomplishments. Look for effort and growth, for a goal that's been reached. Maybe your son didn't get an A on his test, but he studied hard and really tried. Celebrate it! By recognizing these everyday achievements, we are showing love and giving encouragement, which are building blocks to our relationships with one another. Here are a few simple ideas:

Victory jar. Find a clear jar and place it in a highly visible spot in your house. Daily victories can be as simple as doing chores without grumbling, showing compassion, using good table manners, practicing piano without being told, and so on. Maybe there are also more challenging victories, such as modeling Christlike behavior or making the right decision even when it's unpopular. With each "victory" accomplished, write it down on a piece of paper and place it in the jar. Once the jar is full, celebrate together! Make it a movie night, have a special meal, or check out that new place in town.

Pick a meal or dessert night. Select a certain evening of the week. That night for dinner, one person in your family gets to choose the meal or dessert; rotate the person who chooses each week. Choosing a favorite meal or dessert can also be used as a reward for achievement or to honor someone.

Celebration plate. Whenever you want to celebrate or honor someone, use a special "celebration plate," a distinct plate used only for that purpose. Use it for special occasions or to honor good character, kindness, perseverance, or effort. This is such a simple way to make someone feel special without spending money.

Discover Simple Joys

Some days or seasons in life just feel long and discouraging, and it can be hard to break out of that. When my three kids were young and at home, and my husband was putting in long work hours, some of my days would just drag on and the struggles persisted. After one particularly long winter day, I realized I was going to have to bring us out of the funk we were in. I shouted for everyone to get their shoes on and load up. They all looked at me, puzzled, but after a bunch of questions they got in the car. We broke out of the norm that evening by grabbing a donut at a local convenience store and driving around town to look at Christmas lights. Why? Just because! We needed a change of scenery and a reason to turn around our attitudes and focus. It was a great reminder to just do the best we can and celebrate the ordinary days.

Go for ice cream, have a dance party in your living room, set the table extra fancy for your average evening, pick up some fun-themed paper products at the store and have a silly dinner—the possibilities are many.

Appreciate Culture and Travel

Celebrate everyday joys by focusing on other cultures or previous travel experiences you've had. Take the opportunity to learn more about different people groups by trying to incorporate their customs and traditions into your evening. Get your family and friends involved in choosing a culture of interest; research their foods and make them part of your meal. If you have children or grandchildren who are learning about a specific era or historical event in school, integrate that into a celebration to really help them understand what they're learning. I enjoy trying to recapture specific vacations or travel spots through our recipes. For instance, I once tried to re-create a decadent coconut cake my husband and I had in Charleston, South Carolina, for our tenth anniversary. I've also worked together with my kids to try to re-create delicious homemade donuts we ate at the summit of Pikes Peak.

Apron Application

1. If you could celebrate on your next Friday night, what would that look like?

2. What traditions did you grow up with? If you don't still keep those traditions, what new traditions have you started—or could you start—with your friends or family?

3. What is one practical way to find joy in your everyday activities this week?

Prayer

Heavenly Father, thank you for reasons to rest and rejoice. Help me realize the importance of celebrating both big and little accomplishments. Please help me enjoy living life to its fullest with family and friends. Help me show the joy you have given me. Give me ideas of how to enjoy family time even more by developing some habits that lead to fun traditions and memories. In Jesus's name, Amen.

Gather at Your Table

Once you've started finding moments to celebrate (or reward), you can consider ways to make these moments even bigger. Plan ahead by using paper products and/or linens to set up a "theme" night with a tradition or meal your family loves. Research a few other ways to incorporate and learn about another culture while you gather. Perhaps begin by using our menu as a starting point for creating your own Italian pizza party!

— Blueberry & Strawberry Italian Sodas —

Prep time: 20 minutes
Cook time: 20 minutes
Yield: 6 (16 oz.) servings

For the blueberry syrup

1 cup	water
1 cup	sugar
1½ cups	blueberries

For the strawberry syrup

1 cup	water
1 cup	sugar
2 cups	strawberries, hulled

Directions

1. For each batch of syrup, in a medium saucepan, stir together 1 cup water and 1 cup sugar and boil until sugar is completely dissolved.
2. Add blueberries or strawberries and boil for at least 10 minutes, stirring occasionally.
3. Reduce heat and simmer for 10 more minutes. Berries should be mushy.
4. Strain the mixture over a bowl and keep the syrup.
5. Let syrup cool before using. It will stay fresh for a few days in the fridge.

To make the sodas

1 batch	homemade blueberry syrup
1 batch	homemade strawberry syrup
3 liters	club soda
1 pint	half-and-half

Directions

1. Fill a tall glass with ice.
2. Pour 1 part syrup of your choice over ice.
3. Add 3 parts club soda.
4. Add desired amount of half-and-half and stir.
5. Garnish with fresh fruit, if desired.

Denise shares: I have to say the Italian sodas were quite a hit and made the evening even more fun!

Italian Salad

2	large romaine hearts, chopped
1	celery rib, thinly sliced
½	small red onion, thinly sliced
½ cup	cherry tomatoes, halved
¼ cup	pitted black olives
8	pepperoncini
1 cup	Parmigiano-Reggiano cheese, shaved or grated

For the dressing

1	garlic clove, minced
2 Tbs	mayonnaise
2 Tbs	red wine vinegar
½ tsp	dried oregano
6 Tbs	extra virgin olive oil
	salt and freshly ground pepper, to taste

Directions

1. Add all salad ingredients to large serving bowl and combine.
2. Whisk together all dressing ingredients. Just before serving, pour dressing over salad and toss well.
3. Serve immediately.

Cheese Bread

Prep time: 5 minutes
Cook time: 30 minutes
Yield: 12 servings

1 loaf   French bread
1 cup   mayonnaise
½ cup   butter, softened
16 oz.   mozzarella cheese, shredded

Directions

1. Preheat oven to 350°.
2. Cut French bread in half lengthwise and place on a foil-lined baking sheet.
3. Mix mayonnaise, butter, and cheese together and spread evenly on top of bread.
4. Bake until browned and bubbly, approximately 30 minutes.

Lower calorie option: ½ cup mayonnaise, ½ cup butter, and 8 oz. cheese.

Antipasto Platter

Arrange your desired antipasto selection on a tray or board and serve. Here are a few of our favorite options:

cured meats, such as prosciútto, Genoa salami, and pepperoni

garnishes, such as olives, marinated artichoke hearts, and pepperoncini

nuts, such as almonds, cashews, and pistachios

cheeses, such as sun-dried tomato mozzarella, Asiago, pesto-topped Brie, and herb-encrusted goat cheese

homemade bread

assorted crackers

Homemade Pizza Dough

Prep time: 18–20 minutes
+ 1–2 hours rising time
Yield: 1 9x13 or 2 9-inch
round pizza crusts

1 cup	warm water, 100–110°
2¼ tsp	active dry yeast (1 pkg.)
1 Tbs	honey
1¼ tsp	salt
2 Tbs	extra virgin olive oil
3 cups	all-purpose flour

Directions

1. Stir together water, yeast, and honey in large bowl of stand mixer; allow to proof for 5–10 minutes, until foamy.
2. Add salt, oil, and flour and mix until slightly tacky. If needed, add extra flour to achieve the right texture.
3. Switch to a dough hook attachment and knead for about 6 minutes, or knead by hand, until dough is smooth and easy to work with, and sides of bowl should be clean.
4. Place dough in lightly greased bowl, cover with plastic wrap; allow to rise in a warm environment for 1–2 hours or until doubled.
5. Bake dough according to your pizza recipe.

Chicken Alfredo Pizza

Prep time: 15 minutes
Cook time: 10–12 minutes
Yield: 8–10 slices

1 recipe	Homemade Pizza Dough or other pizza crust
½ Tbs	butter
1 Tbs	minced garlic
1 cup	condensed cream of chicken soup
¼ cup	sour cream
¼ cup	milk
1 cup	Parmesan cheese, divided
	salt and pepper, to taste
1–2	cooked chicken breasts, shredded or chopped (rotisserie chicken is wonderful for this recipe)
2 cups	mozzarella cheese, shredded
1	Roma tomato, diced (optional)

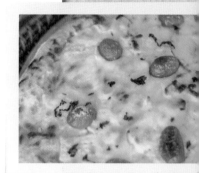

For the sauce

1. Melt butter in a medium saucepan over medium-high heat.
2. Add garlic and lightly brown for 1–2 minutes. Whisk in condensed soup, sour cream, milk, ½ cup Parmesan cheese, and salt and pepper until well combined and warmed through. Remove from heat.

To assemble the pizza

1. Preheat oven to 450°. (If using a pizza stone, place in oven to heat.)
2. Roll dough on a floured surface into a 12-inch circle (for stone) or a large rectangle (for baking sheet). Place on greased pan or hot stone. Cover with sauce, chicken, mozzarella, the remaining Parmesan, and other toppings as desired. Bake for 10–12 minutes.

Annie shares: In the summer, when I don't want to heat up my house with the oven or even when we are entertaining on our deck and want to be outside, we grill our pizzas. We don't have one of those fancy stone pizza ovens built into our backyard, but by using a pizza stone on our very regular gas grill, we create an end product with a very delicious "fired" pizza taste. The bottom becomes just the right amount of charred and the top is bubbly and delicious. We grill the pizza for about 10 minutes over medium-high heat.

Margherita Pizza

Prep time: 10 minutes
Cook time: 20 minutes
Yield: 8–10 slices

1 recipe	Homemade Pizza Dough or other pizza crust
2 cloves	garlic, minced
2 Tbs	olive oil, divided
1 pint	fresh cherry tomatoes, halved
2 sprigs	fresh basil chiffonade
2–3 cups	fresh mozzarella, thinly sliced
¾ cup	Parmesan, grated
	salt and pepper, to taste

Directions

1. Preheat oven to 450°. (If using a pizza stone, place in oven to heat.)
2. Roll out dough and form into desired shape. Let rest for 20 minutes on a pizza peel that has been lightly sprinkled with cornmeal, if desired.
3. In a small skillet, sauté minced garlic in 1 Tbs olive oil for about 1 minute. Add cherry tomatoes. Continue to cook for 5–10 minutes over medium-low heat until tomatoes are soft.
4. When ready to assemble, remove hot pizza stone from oven. Throw on the dough. Add tomatoes (with some of their juice), mozzarella, and Parmesan. Drizzle with 1 Tbs olive oil, then add salt and pepper.
5. Bake for 8–10 minutes. Let cool 5 minutes and sprinkle with basil before serving.

Molly shares: My version of margherita pizza is an effort to replicate the delicious and fresh pizza I once ate among the busy streets in Rome. It will never be exactly the same, but to me it is a memory I can taste through the specific combination of dough, olive oil, garlic, fresh cherry tomatoes, basil chiffonade, a sprinkle of Parmesan—and don't forget the heap of fresh mozzarella.

Hamburger Pizza

Prep time: 20 minutes
Cook time: 15 minutes
Yield: 12-16 squares

1 recipe	Homemade Pizza Dough or other pizza crust
1½–2 lbs.	ground chuck
	salt and pepper, to taste
½ cup	onion, chopped
1	clove garlic, finely chopped
6 oz.	preferred pizza sauce (or crushed tomatoes)
½ cup	onion, chopped (optional)
½ cup	green and red mild peppers, chopped (optional)
2 cups	mozzarella cheese, shredded
½ cup	cheddar cheese, shredded

Directions

1. Preheat oven to 450°. (If using a pizza stone, place in oven to heat.)
2. While dough is rising (see Homemade Pizza Dough recipe, step 4), brown the meat in a large skillet over medium-high heat.
3. Add the salt and pepper, onion, and garlic; simmer on low until beef is thoroughly cooked through and no longer pink.
4. Grease a 10x14 baking sheet. Plop dough onto pan and spread to cover entire pan. You may want to oil or water your hands so the dough doesn't stick.
5. Pour pizza sauce over crust and evenly spread over dough.
6. Using a large spoon, shake hamburger mixture evenly over sauce.
7. Top with chopped veggies, if desired, and cheese.
8. Bake for about 15 minutes or until cheese is browning and bubbly. Cut into squares and enjoy.

Annie shares: This is the pizza Mom made every Friday night when we were kids. It is truly delicious, filling, and comforting. Our favorite side dishes were raw veggies and ranch dressing, potato chips, and fresh fruit. Of course, we kids each got to have our *one* weekly can of pop while we ate it too.

Mocha Brownie Torte

Prep time: 15 minutes
Cook time: 20 minutes
Yield: 12 servings

1	family-sized brownie mix
1 pint	heavy whipping cream
2 Tbs	brown sugar
2 tsp	instant coffee
2 tsp	vanilla extract
1 Tbs	chocolate syrup
1 cup	chopped pecans or black walnuts, optional
	red raspberries or strawberries, to garnish

Directions

1. Place a large mixing bowl and beaters (for a hand mixer) in the freezer to chill.
2. Prepare your favorite boxed brownie mix according to package directions and bake at suggested temperature in 2 prepared (greased and parchment-lined) 8- or 9-inch round cake pans.
3. Remove from pans after 15 minutes and finish cooling on wire rack.
4. Place whipping cream in chilled bowl from freezer and whip on medium speed for 1 minute. Add brown sugar and instant coffee, then continue to beat until stiff peaks form. Fold in vanilla.
5. Place one completely cooled brownie round on a cake stand. Frost only the top with whipped cream frosting.
6. Add second brownie round and frost only the top of that.
7. Drizzle chocolate syrup over torte for garnish.
8. Refrigerate until ready to serve. Serve with chopped nuts and berries to garnish as desired.

Denise shares: This simple recipe is decadent and refreshing, and no one ever guesses that it starts with a brownie mix. You may also frost the entire torte, encasing it in the whipped cream frosting. Sometimes, when I'm in a hurry, I'll pull out the whipped topping.

Cinnamon Streusel Dessert Pizza

Prep time: 20 minutes
Cook time: 9 minutes
Yield: 18 servings

1 recipe	Homemade Pizza Dough or other pizza crust
¾ cup	all-purpose flour
⅓ cup	white sugar
¼ cup	brown sugar
2 tsp	vegetable shortening
1 Tbs	butter, melted
1 tsp	ground cinnamon

For the icing

1 cup	powdered sugar
1 tsp	milk
½ tsp	vanilla

Directions

1. Preheat oven to 450°. (If using a pizza stone, place in oven to heat.)
2. Make the streusel by mixing together flour, sugar, brown sugar, and short-ening with a fork, then side aside. It will be lumpy.
3. To make pizza, roll out dough on a floured surface into a 12-inch circle.
4. Place on preheated stone or greased baking sheet.
5. Perforate dough with a fork (this keeps bubbles from forming), then brush with melted butter.
6. Sprinkle cinnamon over buttered crust.
7. Top with streusel mix.
8. Bake for 8–9 minutes, depending on the thickness of the pizza, until crust is golden brown.
9. Whisk icing ingredients together until they reach drizzling consistency. If it is too thick, thin with a very small additional amount of milk as needed.
10. When pizza has finished baking, top with icing in a circular pinwheel pat-tern. Cut into sticks to serve.

Snow Day

*Choosing an Attitude
of Contentment in All Seasons*

Three-Ingredient Miracle Bread

Hearty Beef Stew

Winter Salad

Gingerbread White Hot Chocolate

Snow Ice Cream (kids' activity)

Fruity Playdough (kids' activity)

Snowball Cupcakes

In Iowa we have the luxury of fully experiencing the four seasons, finding contentment in what the next season has to offer. The new growth and fresh green grass of spring, the heat of summer, the breathtaking changing of the leaves in autumn, and the snowfall of winter. Winter can be an absolutely beautiful time of year here, with blankets of white snow covering the ground, icicles glistening from eaves, and the stillness of the season that offers some reprieve from other busy times in life.

However, there is another side; winter also offers short and gray days, frigid temperatures, and often a sense of isolation. The cold temperatures and snow can linger long into March, and we find ourselves discontent and yearning for the return of spring. The four seasons provide us with divisions of the year, symbolizing the passing of time with changes in weather, daylight, and ecology. Throughout our lives we also experience seasons that resemble different time periods, marked by emotions, circumstances, and conditions.

> *There is a time for everything,*
>   *and a season for every activity under the heavens. (Eccles. 3:1)*

Often in the cold and dark seasons, it is our inherent nature to want to isolate ourselves, stay home, and avoid gathering with others. This may be due to not wanting to brave the cold temperatures and snowy roads or to expose ourselves to all the various germs the season brings, to a case of the winter blues, or to just not wanting to put in the effort. However, we know deep down that the rewards and joy of connecting with one another, especially in an undesirable season of weather or life, are of great value.

On a cold and blustery day, we gathered at Molly's house for our "snow day." We piled out of our vehicles with our laundry baskets overflowing with snow pants, boots, mittens, hats, and scarves. The cousins were all excited to see each other and ran circles around us mothers trying to unload all the items we'd brought for the gathering. The wind was whipping and the snow was blowing, so we figured our time outside would be short. At this stage of life, with small kids, I considered it a victory if we were outside longer than the amount of time it took us to bundle up and prepare to go outside.

All the cousins jumped right into the simple planned activities. They enjoyed snow painting, colored ice cube art design, and throwing lots of snowballs. The children then decided to seek shelter from the elements—not inside, but in their new "fort" under a tall evergreen tree. After playing around a bit under the tree, they decided to expand their fort into the old barn and declared it their "secret hideout," no adults allowed. As we mothers huddled together near the side of the barn to avoid the wind, we could hear lots of giggling and would see an occasional child creep out of the hideout for some fresh snow to eat.

Just as they were starting to tire, Joe arrived on the four-wheeler with multiple sleds attached behind it. This winter event has fondly been called the "sled train," and it is a highlight for all. Huge smiles beamed among the red noses and windburned cheeks, and gleeful shouts of "Faster, Grandpa, faster!" echoed among the trees.

Wet gear and cold little fingers and toes finally won out, and we all headed inside for a comforting warm meal and a few more fun indoor activities. The kids all began with a cup of hot chocolate topped to the brim with marshmallows. Some sat and savored their hot chocolate, while a few got right to work on their playdough creations. We set the food and treats on the table and continued our afternoon together, each enjoying a bowl of comforting and hearty beef stew with a slice of bread slathered with butter. We gathered around the table, connecting with each other over a simple meal and a warm drink, and took turns sharing about the latest happenings in our lives. Most of all, each of us gave a listening ear and a little hope and encouragement to an otherwise monotonous winter day.

While driving home after our day together, I thought winter looked a bit different now. There seemed to be more adventure in the season than before. After a day surrounded by giggles, hot chocolate mustaches, and warm hugs, my heart was full. The connection and the encouragement I felt from being

together with family proved God's faithfulness and his desire for us to be in community and fellowship with one another in all seasons, even the more difficult ones. On that ordinary day in January, all I had to do was fix my mind on the beauty and goodness this winter season provides and garner support and joy from those around me. The light the others provided was a beacon for me in finding contentment on that cold, gray day.

A Place at His Table

Molly

Winter is my least favorite season; I could skip right into spring. I enjoy a fresh snowfall or two and I love Christmas, but after that I'm ready for the next season. Now, for a true farmer, it may be a different story. This is their season to catch up on those to-do lists they've been accumulating all year. The ground is resting, and winter supplies a much-anticipated sigh of relief. I am so thankful for this season because I know how important it is to the vitality of life cycles. I can't have summer all year long, and I understand the winter is good for me too.

My attitude can be changed by my surroundings—the landscape, the temperature, the weather. Then there are factors such as sick children, extra paperwork, a new project deadline, a broken washing machine, or a home renovation that can completely throw any sort of predictability to our day out the window.

This happens to all of us—waves of soaring up and then slowly coming down. It's during these times I can lose my focus on Christ and what he's done for me. Just when I am in high gear, focusing on the ins and outs of the day, I often plainly stumble on a beautiful reminder Jesus lays out before me. There was one day in particular the Lord grabbed hold of me and showed me how powerful he was through the beauty of a magical, frosted, snowy morning. I was in awe of the magnificent sheets of snow blanketing the rolling hills and the encapsulated ice crystals that had formed around each intricate tree branch, leaving no two the same. It seemed I could see every single detail as if under a magnifying lens.

And I felt contentment roll through me.

How could I have lost sight of Christ? How did I so quickly forget to "count my blessings"? It was an awakening for me to not forget his power or neglect to give him my praise. Psalm 37:4 says it so gently:

> Take delight in the LORD,
> and he will give you the desires of your heart.

Although the goodness feels harder for me to find during these less-desirable days, it really doesn't have to be.

Are you in an undesirable season in your life, whether it's winter or something else? Although it may be difficult at times to see the light, with the Lord's help we can still find the good within it. Ask Jesus to help you find the goodness, and "let everything that has breath praise the LORD" (Ps. 150:6). Even during the cold, dark days, Jesus gives us glimpses of beauty—we just have to stop to notice them.

Perhaps your cup is currently filled and overflowing. Then "let your light shine before others, that they may see your good deeds and glorify your Father in heaven" (Matt. 5:16). Think of how you can be the sunshine in someone else's cloudy day. Being around friends or family can be a game-changer when going through sadness or loneliness. I am a true introvert and relish moments of quiet and dreaming—but I can easily lose sight of how much I am invigorated and encouraged by others through gatherings. Don't let your self-doubt or other hindrances keep you from being lifted by others or lifting up others yourself. You will be surprised by how much of a difference you can make!

Key Ingredients

Annie

Make the Decision to Be Content

First Timothy 6:6 says that "godliness with contentment is great gain." And I've learned that when I choose to be content—even in undesirable seasons—I do gain so much fun, rest, and joy, and I make wonderful memories along the way. Whole seasons of the year can be wasted when we stay in a place of discontent. So, how can we practically choose an attitude of contentment? Consider these two simple ideas.

Start your prayer time with thanksgiving. Tell your heavenly Father ten things for which you are truly grateful before asking him to supply any of your needs.

Start a gratitude journal. Inspired by *One Thousand Gifts* by Ann Voskamp, for one year I kept a gratitude journal. Each day, I wrote down three things for which I was thankful. By the end of the year, I had a list of over one thousand blessings. Writing down my blessings helped me train my thoughts to be content and gave me a priceless keepsake.

Let the Season and Your Surroundings Inspire a Gathering

Are you in a winter season in an area where snow abounds? Then run with our snow-day ideas, if you'd like! Other ideas include inviting older kids for a sledding party, gathering teenagers for ice skating or broomball, or joining in with the neighborhood kids in a snowman-building competition. What about trying something new this winter such as cross-country skiing or setting up bird feeders to attract some bright cardinals? My Grandma Betty made winter fun by continuing to make snow angels with her neighborhood friends during their early morning walks into her mid-seventies!

Maybe you live near a beach and can gather together for some sand-castle building, beach volleyball, and a bonfire near the waves. Don't let the thoughts of cleaning up all of those sandy towels and clothes deter you. Gathering amid the sounds of the waves crashing on the shore will be worth any sand cleanup! Check the local sunset time so you can take in an ocean sunset. Do you play guitar, or have a friend who does, and could play music around a beach fire?

If you live in a rainy climate with kids, pull on your best rain gear, do some puddle jumping and snail collecting, then come back inside for a watercolor art activity. My kids and I often use YouTube to watch art tutorials; this is a wonderful resource since you can pause and rewind whenever you need a bit more time or clarification on a step. A rainy-day menu for a gathering in this climate would also naturally include steaming cups of soup and crusty bread.

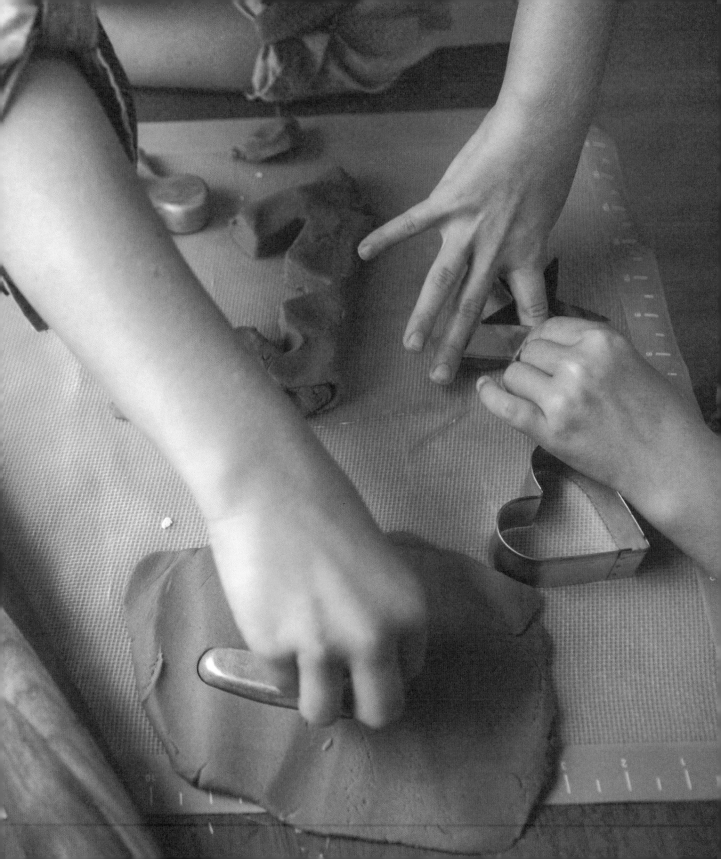

And I think a perfect way to end a meal on a day like that would be to congregate around a fireplace with melty indoor s'mores. Don't you?

Find Contentment through Gathering with Others

When I'm in a difficult season of life, I've found from experience that surrounding myself with family and good friends is a key ingredient to turning my attitude toward one of contentment. After all, God made us for community.

If you don't have family nearby, don't let that deter you from planning a seasonal get-together! Be content with the people in your life, and invite some church friends or neighborhood families. I've learned that when I'm tired of snow or rain or extreme heat, my neighborhood friends are often feeling the same way. We can be a light and a comfort to those around us just by making a little extra effort on an ordinary day.

Apron Application

1. As you read this chapter, what Bible verse(s) caused you to analyze your own attitude?

2. If you were to plan a "snow day," what would it look like? What would your activities be? Who would you invite? What would be on your menu? Take a moment and write those thoughts down.

3. What fond memory would you share if you were headed out for a "snow day" gathering?

Prayer

Thank you, Father, for the many blessings surrounding us and the many blessings we can create for our community as we seek to please you. Please work in and through us to care for others and, by doing so, give you glory. Thank you for your beautiful creation, regardless of where we live and what seasons we encounter. You are God, and you give us so much beauty each and every day; help us see this better by choosing to view life through spiritual lenses. In Jesus's name, Amen.

Gather at Your Table

Fun and *comforting* are two words to describe this gathering. Spending time outdoors doing activities together and then convening in a warm house with a comforting bowl of soup and a slice of bread made our ordinary winter day more enjoyable. Adding easy activities to entertain the younger kids allowed the adults additional time to fellowship while sipping on our decadent hot chocolate.

Three-Ingredient Miracle Bread

Prep time: 5 minutes
Cook time: 50 minutes
Yield: 12 servings

3 cups   self-rising flour
1 cup   sugar
12 oz.   lemon-lime soda (such as Sprite or 7-Up)

Directions

1. Preheat oven to 350°.
2. Mix all ingredients together in a large bowl.
3. Pour into a greased loaf pan.
4. Bake for about 50 minutes or until toothpick inserted in center comes out clean.
5. Remove loaf from pan and allow to cool on a wire rack.

Hearty Beef Stew

Prep time: 30 minutes
Cook time: 2–3 hours
Yield: 6–8 servings

1 lb.   stew beef, cut into small 1-inch chunks
1   bay leaf
2   medium carrots, chopped
1   celery rib, chopped
1 cup   cabbage, chopped
1   small onion, diced
2   large potatoes, peeled and cubed
2 cups   stewed canned tomatoes
1–2 tsp   beef bouillon concentrate
salt and pepper to taste

Directions

1. Place beef stew meat in a large stockpot and cover with water. Add bay leaf and bring to a boil, then lower heat to a simmer until beef is tender, about 2 hours.
2. Add remaining ingredients. Bring back to a boil and simmer until vegetables are tender, approximately 20–30 minutes. Remove bay leaf. Serve.

Winter Salad

Prep time: 5 minutes
Yield: 6 servings

12 oz.	spring mix lettuce
¼ cup	red onion, thinly sliced
⅓ cup	pecan halves
¼ cup	feta or goat cheese, crumbled
2	clementines, peeled and separated
½ cup	fresh blueberries or strawberries
	poppy seed dressing, as desired

Directions

1. Place washed and dried lettuce in a large bowl.
2. Add onion, pecans, feta, and fruit.
3. Drizzle with desired amount of poppy seed dressing or an alternative favorite dressing. Toss and serve.

Gingerbread White Hot Chocolate

Prep time: 2 minutes
Cook time: 10 minutes
Yield: 6 servings

2 cups	milk (or almond milk)
2 cups	half-and-half (or almond milk)
1 cup	white chocolate chips
1 Tbs	maple syrup
1 tsp	vanilla extract
1 tsp	ground cinnamon
½ tsp	ground ginger
⅛ tsp	ground nutmeg
	homemade whipped cream or whipped topping

Directions

1. In a pot over medium heat, combine milk, half-and-half, and white chocolate chips. Whisk continuously until chocolate is fully melted.
2. Add remaining ingredients and stir frequently until heated through.
3. Pour into mugs and top with whipped cream. Sprinkle with additional cinnamon, if desired.

Snow Ice Cream

Prep time: 5 minutes
Yield: 10 servings

8–9 cups	snow, fresh and clean
1 tsp	vanilla extract
1 (14 oz.) can	sweetened condensed milk

Directions

1. Mix all ingredients together in a large bowl.
2. Eat immediately or freeze until serving.

Jenny shares: This is a recipe from Shelby's sister. I have been making it for years, and it has become a wintertime favorite for all—especially my mom! It's fun for my nieces, nephews, and me to go out and collect the snow and mix the ingredients together to have a yummy treat. It's extra delicious topped with fresh fruit and homemade chocolate sauce.

Fruity Playdough

Prep time: 5 minutes
Yield: Enough playdough for about four kids. We often double or triple this recipe.

1 cup + 1 Tbs	all-purpose flour
1 (.14 oz.) pkg.	Kool-Aid (any flavor)
¼ cup	salt
1 Tbs	vegetable oil
⅔–¾ cup	boiling water

Directions

1. Mix all dry ingredients in a bowl until well combined, then add oil.
2. Pour boiling water into flour mixture and mix thoroughly.
3. After it has cooled a little, knead with your hands until smooth.
4. Store in an airtight container for up to 2 months.

Snowball Cupcakes

Prep time: 20 minutes
Cook time: 20–25 minutes
Yield: 24 cupcakes

1½ cups	sugar
¾ cup	butter (1½ sticks), softened
3	eggs
¾ cup	milk
½ cup	water
1 Tbs	vanilla extract
2¾ cups	all-purpose flour
2 Tbs	cornstarch
1 Tbs	baking powder
⅛ tsp	salt

For frosting

8 oz.	cream cheese, softened
1 Tbs	butter
1 tsp	vanilla extract
2 cups	powdered sugar
2 cups	sweetened shredded coconut

Directions

1. Preheat oven to 350°. Line two 12-cup muffin pans with paper liners.
2. In a large bowl, using an electric mixer on medium speed, beat together sugar and ¾ cup butter until creamy.
3. Add eggs one at a time, beating well after each addition.
4. Add milk, water, and 1 Tbs vanilla; beat until combined.
5. In a separate bowl, stir together flour, cornstarch, baking powder, and salt. With the mixer on low speed, gradually add flour mixture to egg mixture, beating until smooth.
6. Divide batter among prepared muffin cups, filling them about two-thirds full.
7. Bake until a toothpick inserted in the center comes out clean, about 20–25 minutes. Let cool on a wire rack for 5 minutes, then remove from pan and cool completely.
8. To make frosting, in a large bowl, whisk together cream cheese, 1 Tbs butter, and 1 tsp vanilla. Add powdered sugar and stir until smooth.
9. Generously frost each cupcake, then sprinkle with shredded coconut. Store in an airtight container until ready to eat.

The Big Game

Treasuring Family
& Spiritual Identity

Oven Roasted Shrimp

Quick & Easy Fruit Pizza

Low-Carb Fruit Pizza

Pulled Pork Sliders & Sauce

Bacon-Wrapped Smokies

Easy Blender Salsa

Layered Chili Cheese Dip

Buffalo Chicken Dip

Caramel Popcorn Balls

What began as a typical annual gathering for our family turned into a night to remember because of one unforgettable TV commercial. Come along with me, on a very cold winter's night, to our snow-covered cozy farmhouse. This house was filled with a cacophony of laughter and cheers, then total silence along with a few tears.

Our *entire* family enjoys sports. All nineteen of us have either played or are currently involved in a sport, and I find having our grandchildren involved in sports brings a whole new dimension to the fun. Our competitive spirits show up as we rally together for our local and professional sports teams. We always look forward to the next game. So it was natural for us Gingham Apron girls to choose the Super Bowl as one of our monthly events.

Along with the pre-game, game, and post-game on the big screen, other games were scattered here and there on our living room carpet atop an endless spread of blankets. We grazed on delicious snacks and appetizers throughout the evening while joining the children in playing checkers, Chutes and Ladders—and dropping in that particular puzzle piece to make a complete scene. While the guys talked about the plays onscreen and their own football days, the gals enjoyed visiting about current happenings and the yummy foods we'd prepared earlier. We shared stories, played games, and opened our hearts to each other. It's a wonderful feeling to have a sense of belonging. And our identity is enriched when we make choices to accept and to love all who come across our path.

Before the game started, each of us voiced which team we were cheering on, but there was something else we loved about the Super Bowl—the unbelievably moving, funny, or exciting commercials. So, at the beginning of the game, we also decided to pay close attention to the commercials and then vote at the end of the night on which one was the best.

As we grabbed more food and talked up a storm, we overheard an announcement onscreen about "the farmer." We all paused, turned our heads to listen, and at once became glued to the commercial on the TV. It was narrated by

Paul Harvey, whom my husband and I were used to hearing from our youth. He eloquently read the poem, "So God Made a Farmer." It described how God made a farmer to care for his precious earth and gave value to the often-hidden hard work that farm life encompasses.

There we were, on our quiet, snow-covered Iowa farm, all cozied in with our eyes glued to the TV, watching and listening to this captivating message about none other than the great American farmer and his way of life. Our family identified with every word as our eyes filled with tears of pride and joy. That was our lifestyle and our heritage, our past and our present, and perhaps our future.

You could have heard a pin drop. What we were hearing and seeing was all true and was the fabric of this family's life, passing the baton from generation to generation. We have deep roots of faith, hard work, and accomplishment. And with each generation, we've taken pride in the responsibility of being caretakers of God's earth and his livestock. This commercial brought back so many memories to Mr. Farmer and me regarding our parents, grandparents, great-grandparents, and so on. We'd grown up hearing stories of hitching up the team of horses to the plow and stories of all the neighbors gathering together to get a crop in, to thresh oats and wheat, and to work the cattle.

The commercial was real, raw, and was about us. Near its end, the little son says he wants to grow up and be just like his dad. I glanced over at my farmer husband, my farmer sons, and our little farmer grandsons. The moment took my breath away; even now it's etched in my mind as if it happened yesterday. At the end of the viewing, we all shouted with broken voices, "That's our favorite Super Bowl commercial!" for we felt truly blessed to be an American farm family.

> *That each of them may eat and drink, and find satisfaction in all their toil—this is the gift of God. (Eccles. 3:13)*

A Place at His Table

Annie

For us, the "So God Made a Farmer" commercial truly celebrated our family. Not only did we get to feel patriotic and proud of being Americans that night, but the message of the commercial, about the importance and weight of the farmer's lifestyle, validated our identity as a farm family. It was touching and wonderful to be able to watch it together.

Do you ever think about the importance of finding and celebrating a group identity? It's wonderful to engage in our culture, to watch for events that are important to our nation, and to use those events as a fun reason to gather. These big games and other events can become catalysts for adding some extra celebration, pride, and richness into our everyday lives. They give us opportunities to gather together with family or community and to build stronger relationships.

While cultural and family identity are important, there is another identity that is even more crucial. That's the identity that can only be found in Christ. God, in his great love, invites us to be adopted into his family, and if we accept this invitation, we become children of God.

> *But when the set time had fully come, God sent his Son . . . to redeem those under the law, that we might receive adoption to sonship. (Gal. 4:4–5)*

> *And I will be a father to you,*
>   *and you shall be sons and daughters to me,*
> *says the Lord Almighty. (2 Cor. 6:18 ESV)*

> *See what great love the Father has lavished on us, that we should be called children of God! (1 John 3:1)*

Jesus came to the world to give us an identity that can never change. He bought us with the price of his blood (1 Cor. 6:20) so that we can be a part of his family forever (John 3:16). I especially love how John 10:29 says that "no one can snatch [us] out of [our] Father's hand." Identity as a child of God can never, ever change.

I've had so many different titles and roles: teacher, athlete, friend, daughter, wife, student, writer, homeschooling mom. And while some of these identities last, many don't endure as life changes. The year before I wrote this I was diagnosed with type 1 diabetes. My identity as a "perfectly healthy, eat anything I want, never get sick" kind of girl was gone in a flash.

The fact that who I am constantly changes has taught me that *whose* I am is more important than *who* I am. If I've built my life on anything other than Christ, I've built my life on the sand, not on the rock of Jesus (Matt. 7:24–27). But if my identity is placed in him, then "[my] life is now hidden with Christ in God" (Col. 3:3), and what really matters can't ever change.

If you belong to Christ, if you've given your life to him and he is your Lord, then celebrate it! Think about the immeasurable impact your identity as his child has had on your life. He's given you the gifts of peace, security, and unconditional love.

And if you have never placed your faith in Christ and joined God's family? Oh, friend, Jesus is calling you to follow him, and as 2 Corinthians 6:2 says, "'In the time of my favor I heard you, and in the day of salvation I helped you.' I tell you, now is the time of God's favor, now is the day of salvation." So, what should be your first step? I suggest starting by reading the book of John in the New Testament, asking God to direct you to a solid, Bible-believing church, and even contacting us through our website, The Gingham Apron. This book could truly reach no greater goal than to invite you into a new identity with Christ, so you can join us in claiming this verse for yourself:

> I have been crucified with Christ and I no longer live, but Christ lives in me. The life I now live in the body, I live by faith in the Son of God, who loved me and gave himself for me. (Gal. 2:20)

Let's celebrate our beautiful cultural and unique family identities with wonderful gatherings, big games, and delicious fun food. These are from God! But let's first find our true meaning, worth, and security in belonging to Christ.

Key Ingredients

Shelby

We who have received Christ as our Savior are all children of God (John 1:12). We also each have our earthly backgrounds and distinctive stories that make up part of who we are. Let's look at some ways we can celebrate who we are and our identities together, along with serving and honoring the Lord.

Discover Heritage

Our heritage often includes cultural aspects and traditions that have been passed down through generations of family or community. There are many ways to celebrate that. These ideas are a good starting point.

Create a family tree. If you have access, find out about your ancestors or older generations in your current family. What are their names? Where did they live? How many children did they have? Looking at family history is a wonderful way to better understand diversity and keep memories alive. See the richness in how God has moved through your family.

Educate yourself. What are some interesting facts about your cultural background? If you haven't already, take time to learn the history, culture, and traditions of that specific country or countries and regions.

Explore and engage. Make exploring fun; find a local festival to attend or watch a movie that relates to your heritage. Cook foods associated with your heritage. Draw closer to your geographical roots with some new dishes for your family.

Incorporate cultural traditions. Did a certain tradition from your cultural background spark interest in you as you learned about it? Try incorporating it into your family, perhaps beginning with a gathering. Invite over a neighbor or two, host a backyard gathering, and have each attendee bring something specific to their own diverse background. Celebrate each other and your differences.

Create a sense of belonging. In a world that is full of hurt and misunderstanding, we can lose our sense of belonging and at times our identity. What are ways you can help others feel like they belong? What reminders could help them remember they are brothers and sisters in Christ? Invite them over for coffee. Make them feel welcome. Extend an invitation to that extra person when a group is already gathering. Send an encouraging note with Scripture included, and share a piece of God's love.

Apron Application

Molly

1. Our spiritual identity as children of God is our most important identity to celebrate. Spend some quiet time in prayer and read through the Gospel of John. Prepare your heart so it is ready to receive.

   Confess and repent. First John 1:9 says, "If we confess our sins, he is faithful and just and will forgive us our sins and purify us from all unrighteousness."

   Trust. As it is spelled out in Romans 10:9, "If you declare with your mouth, 'Jesus is Lord,' and believe in your heart that God raised him from the dead, you will be saved."

   Receive. The power of the Holy Spirit lives in and through you. You are covered in God's grace. Isaiah 1:18 says, "Though your sins are like scarlet, they shall be as white as snow; though they are red as crimson, they shall be like wool."

2. What challenges and difficulties are you facing in your life right now? Write them down and lay them at the feet of Jesus. Be reminded that God is in complete control, and although life continually changes around us, our Lord Jesus is a solid rock who never changes. Don't forget *whose* you are.

3. Reflect upon your own identity. What makes you unique? What do you enjoy? In what ways can you use your inherited character qualities as you live out your role of a Christ-follower? What is something you've learned about your own heritage or someone else's?

Prayer

Heavenly Father, what a blessing and an honor it is to be a part of your eternal kingdom. Thank you for the free gift of your Son, Jesus, and that we get to be a part of your forever family. Thank you for loving us and giving us grace by transforming our sin to be as white as snow. Please help us remember that we are yours, and you are our solid rock. Help us use our unique qualities and our heritage to glorify and honor you. In Jesus's name, Amen.

Gather at Your Table

Whether you gather around the TV, host a game night, or just get together with friends and family, we think you will enjoy these delicious appetizers and finger foods. This particular night was fun and festive, as a party should be. If children are attending, we encourage you to be equipped with special toys they can play with such as LEGOs or dominos. We also brought out some favorite soft drinks to go with our party foods.

Oven Roasted Shrimp

Prep time: 10 minutes
Cook time: 15 minutes
Yield: 8 servings

½ cup butter (1 stick)
1 lemon, sliced
2 lbs. fresh shrimp, peeled and deveined
1 pkg Italian dressing mix

Directions

1. Preheat oven to 350°.
2. Melt butter in a rimmed baking sheet while the oven preheats.
3. Layer lemon slices on top of melted butter.
4. Spread fresh shrimp on top, and sprinkle with Italian seasoning.
5. Roast for 15 minutes.

Quick & Easy Fruit Pizza

Prep time: 15 minutes
Cook time: 12 minutes
Yield: 16 servings

1 (17.5 oz.) pouch sugar cookie mix
½ cup butter, softened (1 stick)
1 egg
8 oz. cream cheese, softened
7 oz. marshmallow creme
2-3 cups fruit of your choice, chopped into small pieces

Directions

1. Preheat oven to 350°.
2. Combine sugar cookie mix with butter and egg, mix well.
3. Using your hands, spread the dough evenly on a large baking sheet. Prick the dough all over with a fork to prevent air bubbles. Bake until lightly browned, about 12 minutes. Remove from oven and cool completely.
4. Beat together cream cheese and marshmallow creme until smooth, and frost the cookie dough "crust." Cover the pizza with fruit.
5. Refrigerate until serving. Slice into squares.

Low-Carb Fruit Pizza

Prep time: 20 minutes
Cook time: 12–14 minutes
Chill time: 2 hours
Yield: 8 servings

For the crust

1¼ cups	almond flour
⅓ cup	granular erythritol
1 tsp	baking powder
1	egg
5 Tbs	butter, softened
1 tsp	vanilla

For the topping

6 oz.	cream cheese (or Neufchâtel)
2 Tbs	granular erythritol
1 Tbs	heavy whipping cream
½ cup	fresh strawberries, sliced
½ cup	fresh blueberries

Directions

1. Preheat oven to 350° and grease the bottom of a 9-inch springform pan.
2. In a medium bowl, whisk together almond flour, erythritol, and baking powder. Add egg, butter, and vanilla and stir until well combined.
3. Spread in the prepared pan, pressing down evenly, and bake for 12–14 minutes, until lightly browned. Allow crust to cool completely before releasing it from the pan.
4. Mix cream cheese, erythritol, and cream until completely combined. Spread evenly over cooled crust. Garnish with fresh berries.
5. Cover and refrigerate for at least 2 hours before serving.

Annie shares: I have type 1 diabetes, so I need to limit my sugar intake. This low-sugar fruit pizza recipe features bright flavors and beautiful design—it's a delightful alternative to our family's traditional fruit pizza recipe.

Pulled Pork Sliders & Sauce

Prep time: 15 minutes
Cook time: 3 hours
Yield: 10–12 servings

3 lbs. pork roast
10–12 slider buns

For the sauce

1 clove garlic, minced
1 Tbs butter
½ cup ketchup
⅓ cup chili sauce
2 Tbs brown sugar
2 Tbs chopped onion
1 Tbs Worcestershire sauce
1 Tbs prepared mustard
1 Tbs celery seed
¼ tsp salt
dash hot pepper sauce

Directions

1. Roast pork in oven for approx. 3 hours at 325° or in slow cooker for 5–6 hours on low, until pork is tender.
2. Pull pork apart using two forks.
3. In oven-safe skillet or large saucepan, sauté garlic in butter.
4. Add remaining sauce ingredients and bring to boil, then simmer for 20–30 minutes.
5. Stir sauce into shredded pork and return to oven or slow cooker to heat through, about 20 minutes.
6. Fill your favorite slider buns with meat and sauce.

Bacon-Wrapped Smokies

1 lb. bacon
1 (16 oz.) pkg. Lit'l Smokies sausages
1 cup brown sugar

Prep time: 15 minutes
Cook time: 30 minutes
Yield: 30 smokies

Directions

1. Preheat oven to 350°.
2. Cut bacon into thirds and wrap each strip around a sausage. Use a wooden toothpick to secure bacon.
3. Arrange smokies on baking sheet and sprinkle liberally with brown sugar (or use a plastic bag to shake and coat them).
4. Bake until bacon is crisp and brown sugar is melted, about 30 minutes, rotating halfway through cooking.

Easy Blender Salsa

¾ cup red onion, chopped
½ cup fresh cilantro, minced
1 (10 oz.) can diced tomatoes with green chiles, undrained
1 (10 oz.) can diced tomatoes with lime juice and cilantro, undrained
1 clove garlic
1 jalapeño (seeded according to heat preference)

Prep time: 5 minutes
Yield: 10–12 servings

Directions

1. Place all ingredients in blender and process until smooth. Refrigerate until ready to serve.
2. Serve with tortilla chips. (Warm chips at 350° for 4–5 minutes for more of a restaurant experience!)

Layered Chili Cheese Dip

Prep time: 5 minutes
Cook time: 5 minutes
Yield: 10 servings

8 oz.   cream cheese, softened
1 (15 oz.) can   chili (with or without meat, your preference)
1½ cups   shredded cheddar cheese

Optional toppings

chopped onion
sliced black olives

Directions

1. Spread cream cheese with a rubber spatula to cover the entire bottom of a 9- or 12-inch serving dish.
2. Empty can of chili on top of cream cheese, and spread evenly.
3. Sprinkle shredded cheese evenly over chili layer.
4. Microwave in 30-second intervals until cheese is melted thoroughly.
5. Top with optional toppings as desired.
6. Serve with corn chips or tortilla chips.

Buffalo Chicken Dip

Prep time: 5 minutes
Cook time: 20–25 minutes
Yield: 12 servings

16 oz.   cream cheese
1 cup   ranch dressing
¾–1 cup   hot sauce (depending on how spicy you like it)
2 (10 oz.) cans   chunk chicken, drained, or 1½ cups shredded cooked chicken
1 cup   shredded cheddar cheese

Directions

1. Preheat oven to 350°.
2. Spray 9x13 pan with nonstick spray.
3. Mix cream cheese, ranch, and hot sauce together, then stir in chicken.
4. Pour into pan and sprinkle with shredded cheese.
5. Bake for 20–25 minutes until heated through and cheese is melted and bubbly.
6. Serve with tortilla chips, celery sticks, or chicken-flavored crackers.

Caramel Popcorn Balls

Prep time: 10 minutes
Cook time: 10 minutes
Yield: 15 mini popcorn balls

8 cups	popped popcorn
¾ cup	sugar
¾ cup	brown sugar
½ cup	light corn syrup
½ cup	water
1 tsp	white vinegar
¼ tsp	salt
¼ cup	butter (½ stick)

Directions

1. Place popcorn in a very large mixing bowl.
2. Combine remaining ingredients, except for butter, in a large saucepan. Heat to boiling over medium-high heat. Cook, stirring constantly, to hard ball stage or 260° if using a candy thermometer.
3. Remove from heat and stir in butter until melted.
4. Pour syrup in a thin stream over popcorn while mixing it into the popcorn. (We like to ask for help while performing this little task.) Stir well, covering all the popcorn.
5. Butter your hands and form popcorn balls. (We prefer mini popcorn balls.)

Home

A Poem

The following poem was discovered one day, handwritten on a piece of weathered paper, in an antique clock that once belonged to our Grandma Maxine's parents. The message of this poem, author unknown to us, is a beautiful reminder of the blessings of a godly home.

A window where a lamp beckons you

The arms of a love, precious, and true

A haven at the end of the day

A castle, I have heard men say

A flower that grows about

A shade from a tree tall and stout

Children that play on the lawn

A whisper that awakens you at dawn

The noise that children make

The fragrance of oven fresh cake

A book and an old easy chair

A reason to love and to share

A blessing from the Almighty One

A Special Invitation

We invite you to have a relationship with Christ. This "Romans Road" is one of many tools used to show us the steps to accepting Christ Jesus as our personal Savior and Lord.

1. Romans 3:23. "All have sinned and fall short of the glory of God." Everyone who has been born has a sin problem that keeps us distant from a holy God. Nothing we can do can wash away our sins . . . nothing.

2. Romans 6:23. "For the wages of sin is death, but the gift of God is eternal life in Christ Jesus our Lord." Jesus provided a way for us to escape eternal death without God: a free gift of eternal life if we recognize our need and reach out to receive it.

3. Romans 5:8. "But God demonstrates his own love for us in this: While we were still sinners, Christ died for us." Only the blood of the sacrificial Lamb can wash away our sins.

4. Romans 10:9–10. "If you declare with your mouth, 'Jesus is Lord,' and believe in your heart that God raised him from the dead, you will be saved. For it is with your heart that you believe and are justified, and it is with your mouth that you profess your faith and are saved." When this decision takes place, you are no longer an enemy of God but his child (John 1:12) and a new creation (2 Cor. 5:17). It begins the moment

you trust Jesus Christ to take away your sins and ask him to be your Savior. At this time, the Holy Spirit comes to dwell inside of you, to council and guide you.

5. Romans 10:13. "Everyone who calls on the name of the Lord will be saved." You can *know*, without a doubt, that you have eternal life and are assured of salvation.

Prayer

Lord Jesus, I understand now that I am a sinner, which separates me from you. I am sorry for the wrong I have done in this life, and I ask that you please forgive me. I realize only you, Jesus, have the power to cleanse me and give me new life through your shed blood. Please come into my life and save me. I want to no longer be a child of this world but a child of yours. In Jesus's name I pray, Amen.

Acknowledgments

We would like to thank:

Our husbands, for supporting us since the beginning of our original "cookbook idea," and for graciously enduring many pieces of pie and an unforgettable family photoshoot among the chiggers.

Our children, for keeping the gatherings fun and full of laughter, along with willingly (most of the time) wearing the requested clothes, some itchy and some too warm for the photoshoots.

Special thanks to Grandma Lorilyn and Granny Cath, for always believing in and willingly participating in our project. Your support, whether it was becoming our first email subscriber, documenting our journey in a special scrapbook, or managing children behind the scenes, has provided continual encouragement from the very beginning.

Katie Swanson Photography, for coming alongside our family and beautifully capturing our gatherings, along with adding an extra element of humor and lightheartedness. You were terrific!

Most importantly, though, we have our heavenly Father to thank. If it weren't for his love for us, there would not be a desire to have written this book. We are truly grateful for our lives in him through his Son, Jesus Christ.

Notes

Family Picnic at the Park

1. C. H. Spurgeon, "'The Lord Is My Shepherd'," sermon 3006, Spurgeon Gems, accessed January 27, 2020, https://www.spurgeongems.org/sermon/chs3006.pdf.
2. Erica Orange, Jared Weiner, and Eshanthi Ranasinghe, "A Mental Health Pandemic: Is the World Getting More Addicted, Anxious, and Lonely?" Omidyar Network, March 19, 2019, https://www.omidyar.com/blog/mental-health-pandemic-world-getting-more-addicted-anxious-and-lonely.

Tea Party

1. Anne Ortlund, *The Gentle Ways of the Beautiful Women*, vol. 1: *Disciplines of the Beautiful Woman* (Waco, TX: Word, 1984).

Anniversary Picnic & Bike Ride

1. C. H. Spurgeon, "Psalm 77:11," *Treasury of David* (Bible Study Steps, 2016), ebook.
2. Robert Robinson, "Come, Thou Fount of Every Blessing," 1758.
3. Taken in part from "5 Reasons You Should Celebrate Milestones," First Things First, accessed March 10, 2020, https://firstthings.org/5-reasons-you-should-celebrate-milestones.

Hayride, Easy Sunday Supper & Bonfire

1. Taken in part from "5 Basic Needs to Survive and Thrive," Santevia, accessed April 3, 2019. https://www.santevia.com/blog/5-basic-needs-to-survive-and-thrive/.
2. Macmillan Thesaurus, s.v. "Feelings of Love, Respect and Admiration," accessed April 3, 2019, https://www.macmillandictionary.com/thesaurus-category/british/feelings-of-love-respect-and-admiration.

Recipe Index

About the Authors

You can find The Gingham Apron family at www.theginghamapron.com.

Annie Boyd is Denise's daughter and the wife of Shane, her high school sweetheart. She is the mother of five gregarious and adventurous children, whom she homeschools. She loves traveling, spending time outside, reading, and baking bread. Annie received her BA in elementary education and biblical studies from the University of Northwestern, St. Paul. She accepted Christ as a young girl and hopes to invite others to know about his love, faithfulness, and forgiveness.

Shelby Herrick is married to Denise's oldest son, Bill. Although she comes from a long lineage of Iowa farmers who trace back over multiple generations, Shelby never envisioned she would be living a rural life. But God always has a plan! These days you can find her living on a farm with her husband, three fun-loving kiddos, and a multitude of animals. Shelby is a follower of Christ and enjoys spending time with loved ones, digging into the Word with friends, vacationing with her family, and exercising. Shelby has both an undergraduate degree in corporate wellness and a master's degree in education from Northwest Missouri State University.

Molly Herrick is Denise's daughter-in-law, married to Joe. They have two enthusiastic, adventurous children. They live on a century-old farmstead and produce crops and raise cattle. Growing up, she would have never dreamed of marrying a farmer. Molly graduated from Iowa State University with a degree in interior design, and spent a semester studying in Rome, Italy. Molly loves God and people and believes in the importance of hospitality. She is continually inspired by nature and loves to be outdoors when she's not designing, decorating, and trying new recipes.

Jenny Herrick is Denise's youngest daughter. She has always loved country living and is especially intrigued by all the animals, from farm animals to Midwest wildlife. Her golden retriever, Maggie, has brought much happiness to not only Jenny but the entire family. Jenny loves to travel, to hang out with family and friends, and to see a heartwarming movie or theater performance. She enjoys working with children at the local elementary school, and she ministers to the youth through her church, along with other duties. She dedicated her life to the Lord as a child and has grown up in the church, enjoying rich fellowship.

Denise Herrick is the mother and mother-in-law of these four blessed young women, and she is privileged to be a slice of The Gingham Apron. She is an Iowa farm wife who treasures her devoted husband of more than forty-five years and is the mom and mom-in-law to three men whom she admires greatly for their devotion to God, family, and a strong work ethic. Grandma of ten beautiful gifts, she delights in spending time with them and hopes to inspire them to love the Lord. A devoted follower of Christ, Denise loves spending time learning about her Savior. She also loves serving at her church, especially in women's and children's ministries. Denise enjoys people, adventure, and travel. She is inspired by listening to podcasts and reading books that build up her faith as she tends her lawn and flower gardens, passionately cooks, and helps out on the farm.

GET TO KNOW

The Gingham Apron!

More recipes, blog posts, and info at

TheGinghamApron.com

theginghamapron